FOR THIS
I WAS BORN

FOR THIS
I WAS BORN

Brian Houston

THOMAS NELSON
Since 1798

NASHVILLE   DALLAS   MEXICO CITY   RIO DE JANEIRO   BEIJING

Published in Nashville, Tennessee, by Thomas Nelson. Thomas Nelson is a trademark of Thomas Nelson, Inc.

Thomas Nelson, Inc., titles may be purchased in bulk for educational, business, fund-raising, or sales promotional use. For information, please e-mail SpecialMarkets@ThomasNelson.com.

Unless otherwise noted, Scripture quotations are taken from THE NEW KING JAMES VERSION. © 1982 by Thomas Nelson, Inc. Used by permission. All rights reserved.

Scripture quotations marked AMP are from THE AMPLIFIED BIBLE: OLD TESTAMENT. ©1962, 1964 by Zondervan (used by permission); and from THE AMPLIFIED BIBLE: NEW TESTAMENT. © 1958 by the Lockman Foundation (used by permission).

Scripture quotations marked KJV are from KING JAMES VERSION of the Bible.

Scripture quotations marked MSG are from *The Message* by Eugene H. Peterson. © 1993, 1994, 1995, 1996, 2000. Used by permission of NavPress Publishing Group. All rights reserved.

Scripture quotations marked NIV are from HOLY BIBLE: NEW INTERNATIONAL VERSION®. © 1973, 1978, 1984 by International Bible Society. Used by permission of Zondervan Publishing House. All rights reserved.

Scripture quotations marked NLT are from *Holy Bible*, New Living Translation. © 1996. Used by permission of Tyndale House Publishers, Inc., Wheaton, Illinois 60189. All rights reserved.

Library of Congress Cataloging-in-Publication Data

Houston, Brian.
    For this I was born / Brian Houston.
        p. cm.
    Includes bibliographical references and index.
    ISBN 978-0-8499-1913-8
    1. Life—Religious aspects—Christianity. I. Title.
BT696.H68 2008
248.4—dc22   2008003185

Printed in the United States of America

08 09 10 11 12 RDD 5 4 3 2 1

To all those past and present who have made the choice to live for the cause of Jesus Christ and put the kingdom first in everything they do.

Contents

CONTENTS

Acknowledgments

I HAVE A LOT OF VALUABLE PEOPLE IN MY LIFE who share my passion for Jesus and his church. Primary among them is Bobbie, my beautiful wife, and each of our adult children who share my passion for Christ's cause. I love them.

Thank you to Maria Ieroianni, for her belief in this project and her commitment to seeing it become a reality, and to the other wonderful staff who helped review and edit this book over many months.

And to our whole team, whose selfless commitment to the cause enables Hillsong Church to be and to bless others.

Prologue

EACH MORNING WHEN I WAKE UP, ALTHOUGH I may agonize over whether to go for a run, I do not wonder what I should do with my life. That was determined when I was a young boy. I grew up the son of a minister, and from about the age of five, I developed a real sense that I was born for something bigger than myself—I wanted to be a leader and build the church—to do something for the kingdom of God that made a difference.

Don't get me wrong; I had no real clue what being a leader and building the church was going to entail, nor did I realize the opportunities and challenges that would come along the way, but through all of life's journey thus far, that desire has resonated in my spirit.

Nevertheless, more than half a century of life and more than thirty years of ministry have taught me that my experience is not everyone else's experience. Perhaps you have struggled with the questions of why you are alive, what life is all about, and the part you play in it. Maybe you have pursued material things, unhealthy relationships, or found solace in alcohol and drugs in the hope of finding fulfillment, only to realize that there must be more to life.

I am here to tell you that there is! You have a Father in heaven who has marked you for his purpose and plan. You were born for a cause that embraces humanity but resonates from heaven. It is a cause that bridges history and alters eternity.

Your life is not a result of powerless fate. It is attached to a predetermined purpose that originated in the mind of the Father. For some this is a totally foreign concept, while for others this revelation already burns in your heart. Whatever has compelled you to pick up this book, my hope is that the God-truths, wisdom, and personal lessons contained within its pages will help propel you to a greater understanding of the cause of the King and the kingdom and the unique part you play.

Jesus himself taught us to seek first the kingdom of God. The kingdom is not a mystical place in the heavens; it is everything in the realm of Christ. Having kingdom purpose involves bringing the will of heaven to earth. Kingdom purpose is a revelation that will change your life and has the power to impact the life of everyone you encounter.

Time and again I have seen how the cause of Christ has taken the hopeless and filled them with hope, and grabbed hold of the purposeless and infused them with purpose. And suddenly their lives make sense. My prayer is that you also can say with conviction, "For this cause, I was born!"

SECTION 1

FOR THIS CAUSE I WAS BORN

Chapter 1

You Were Born
for the Cause of Christ

TIME IS TICKING. EACH OF US WILL WALK THE planet for a certain number of days; we all have a specific number of breaths and heartbeats to expend. The question is: what will you do with the years, months, weeks, days, and minutes God has given you?

What cause, if any, will define your life? How will you be remembered? What legacy will you leave for your family and the generations to come? The answers rest with you.

In the midst of a society often defined by skepticism and cynicism, everyone contemplates and searches for answers and something to believe in. There are no limits to causes, both positive and negative, that vie for our commitment, passion, money, and time. We have our families, our mortgages, our work. And then there are the global causes of injustice, inequity, the fight against terrorism, climate change, the list is endless.

I wholeheartedly believe there is one cause that is greater than any other, a cause that when lived to fulfillment impacts every area of our lives. It gives meaning, direction,

> *I wholeheartedly believe there is one cause that is greater than any other*

and purpose to every day; it influences your choices and decisions; it sets your children up to win; and it has the potential to affect all who cross your path.

It is the cause of Jesus Christ. There is no greater cause on the planet.

To understand the power of this cause, we have to look to the life of Jesus himself. Some two thousand years ago, he—an innocent man—stood in front of a judge and faced a barrage of questions that would determine whether he lived or died a horrible death. His is perhaps the most notorious trial in recorded history. To this day it sparks controversy and is the subject of many books and movies. Jesus did not have a vast legal team advising him on what to say or how to plead; in fact, he refused to defend himself against the injustice he suffered. Instead, he declared a truth so absolute that it confounded all who were present.

A weak Roman governor, desperate to appease the blood-thirsty crowd, asked a probing question of Jesus: "Are you a king then?" And he received a powerful, definitive answer:

> You say rightly that I am a king. *For this cause* I was born, and *for this cause* I have come into the world. (John 18:37, emphasis added)

"For this cause" is a statement of certainty and conviction. Jesus Christ knew exactly who he was, and the purpose for which he was alive was unmistakable. His was a cause so vital that he would willingly die for it.

Speaking of his impending death on a cross, Jesus declared, "For this cause, I came unto this hour" (John 12:27 KJV). His entire life was encapsulated in that one powerful phrase—"for this cause."

Do you have such boldness and certainty when it comes to life's big questions? Why were you born? Why are you on the planet at this time in history?

It has been said, "Everyone who is born dies, but not everyone who dies has truly lived." God does not want you and me to die full of potential. He wants you to live for something worth dying for. When Christ's cause truly underpins your life, you will discover meaning and purpose, and your life will never be the same again.

Why are you on the planet at this time in history?

Born Because

I was blessed to be in the delivery room for the birth of each of our amazing children: Joel, Ben, and Laura. I marveled at the miracle unfolding before me, and particularly at my wife, Bobbie's, pain threshold! I will never forget the feeling of sheer exhilaration as I held each baby for the first time. As their big eyes looked up at me, trying to make sense of this new, womb-free world they had entered into, I prayed over their God-given futures.

We all enter the world the same way—well, relatively. We have a mom; most of us are born in a hospital; we experience the shock of elevated noise and light levels. On the other hand, the circumstances we're born into may differ significantly. Perhaps yours were less than ideal. It is possible you never had a dad who prayed over your future, and maybe the family situation you were born into was not perfect or you were unwanted.

Coming to grips with the truth that you were born for a cause greater than yourself may be difficult. Your past, your family upbringing, and your choices to this point may have you convinced that your lot is settled and there is no way things can get any better.

I am here to tell you, as simply as I can, that there is a "because" factor in your life. You were born because the Father has a plan for you on the earth. He has a purpose for you that transcends your family, your upbringing, and your mistakes. It is greater than the limitations of your environment or the challenges of your circumstances.

Hillsong Church, the church Bobbie and I planted in 1983 and still pastor, is filled with extraordinary people and amazing stories, but not all of them had a great start. We have a dynamic and gifted leader in our church whose unwavering passion is to see people switched on to the cause of Christ. Today she travels the globe as a sought-after communicator. But go back some two decades, and you would encounter an angry young woman in her early twenties, wrestling with issues that stem from a strict Greek Orthodox heritage, sexual abuse, and a sense of inferiority because of her socioeconomic background.

Giving her life to Jesus Christ gave her the sense of direction and purpose that only comes with knowing she has an awesome, God-given destiny to fulfill. Christine became actively involved in our church youth group, and her life

7

started on the course that has enabled her to go and do what she once only could have imagined.

Yet her story does not end there. Prior to her thirty-third birthday, she discovered she had been adopted at birth. This startling news came as a huge shock, and it could easily have thrown her off course and caused her to question her identity. But she never wavered from her sense of destiny and purpose. Regardless of the circumstances of her birth, Christine knew she was alive for the cause of the King and the kingdom. Nothing could ever change that.

I do not know what the circumstances of your birth or upbringing were, but they do not change one very potent truth: before you were born, the Father knew you, destined you, and purposed you.

In the Bible, God tells us, "Before I formed you in the womb I knew you; before you were born I sanctified you" (Jer. 1:5). David declared to the Lord, "You formed my inward parts; You covered me in my mother's womb" (Ps. 139:13).

> *You were born for the cause of the King and the kingdom.*

You were created by God on purpose, and He has a plan for you. You were born for the cause of the King and the kingdom.

Against All Odds

If you still are not convinced, consider the less-than-ideal circumstances surrounding the birth of Jesus. In today's society he almost certainly would be classified as coming from a dysfunctional background. First, he was born to a young teenage girl who, at the time of conception, was not even married. Second, the man she married, Joseph, was not actually his biological father. Third, his *real* father was an unusual entity. Imagine Jesus as a young boy trying to explain to the other children in his village who his dad was. How difficult would it have been explaining to his friends that his father was actually God himself?

There are many other circumstances surrounding his actual birth that could be described as abnormal. His mother was whisked off to another town for his birth, and he was instantly pursued by a paranoid king. He certainly was not born in a sterilized hospital delivery room, surrounded by the comforts of life. We often create images of cozy nativity scenes on Christmas cards, but the reality was a stable most likely infested by rats and vermin and an all-enveloping stench! From early childhood Jesus was faced with the enormous pressure of expectation. The Scriptures declared that "the government shall be upon his shoulder" (Isa. 9:6 KJV), so Jesus had a lot to live up to. The Bible also says that when

Jesus was born the angels sang, "Peace to *all* men and women on earth who please him" (Luke 2:14 MSG, emphasis added). But not "all men and women" responded gladly to Him. He was despised, mocked, and condemned to death. Jesus had to deal with the pain of rejection, yet that did not hold him back.

Some of us may be ruled by the experience of betrayal or broken trust. Jesus too was betrayed; in fact, it was at the hands of one in his closest circle of friends. Jesus also faced continual persecution from the Pharisees wherever he went. The bombardment of religious legalism and persecution probably would have immobilized most of us, yet he rose above every challenge and obstacle.

Jesus did not live out his life from a position of insecurity, negativity, or rejection, because he knew he was on earth for his Father's cause.

In human terms, Jesus had plenty of reasons to fail in life, but two thousand years later his birth, his life, and his death continue to impact the world. It was not the circumstances of his birth or the opinions of people that determined his purpose or direction. He did not live out his life from a position of insecurity, negativity, or rejection, because he knew he was on earth for his Father's cause. This sense of cause put *everything*—especially the tough times—in perspective.

Living with a sense of cause equally applies to you. Once you understand the power of Christ's cause, everything else falls into place. It is at that point that you start becoming all that the Lord has called you to be. Instead of being ruled by the circumstances of your birth or the limitations of your background, you can move forward into God's amazing plan for your life.

> *Instead of being ruled by the circumstances of your birth or the limitations of your background, you can move forward into God's amazing plan for your life.*

Certain bad things may have happened in your past, but the power of those negative situations can be broken so that it does not affect you today.

I encourage you to allow the reality that you were born for an awesome reason to penetrate your heart. It will help give you a new perspective, a God-perspective. Go to the Word and let the promises of the Lord permeate your soul. Renew your mind (Rom. 12:2), develop a fresh way of thinking, and start seeing yourself as the Lord sees you. I know from experience that there is no richer reward in life than discovering God's purpose and allowing it to fuel your vision and direction.

Bobbie and I are blessed to pastor Hillsong Church, which in my biased view is a great church. For more than two decades it has grown in size, influence, and effectiveness. But if you had met me at seventeen, you would not have nominated me to be in the "most likely to succeed" category. Although I was blessed to have a great family, four brothers and sisters, a wonderful and loving mum, and a hero for a dad, I was an awkward teenager. I was not a great student, and I blinked incessantly whenever I got up to preach. But deep down I somehow knew that I was alive for a purpose that was bigger than I was, and gradually I started to gain the unfolding revelation of what I believed I was put on the earth to do.

A lesson I learned as a young man at Bible college, and one that has never left me, is that no matter what occurs in life, you should never allow yourself to develop a wounded spirit. As a result, I have never looked at my life in terms of what I lack or what happened to me in the past, but according to the knowledge that I was born for the cause of the King and the kingdom. This mind-set has equipped me to confront and rise above inadequacies, lack, and feelings likely to limit or contain me. I have been confronted by some extraordinary twists in life, but I know with certainty that my foundation is Jesus!

So why are you on earth today? It was not the luck of the

draw. Think about this: you are a one-in-a-million success story from the moment of your conception. There is no mistake about who you are and who you are destined to be. When you get a revelation of this fact, no matter what comes against you in life, it will not be able to throw you off course.

Knowing that you were born for a cause will keep you moving forward and release you into the plans and purposes of the Father.

> *I have never looked at my life in terms of what I lack . . . but according to the knowledge that I was born for the cause of the King and the kingdom.*

Chapter 2

Championing the Cause
of the Local Church

LOVE IS A FUNNY THING. IT CAN MAKE PEOPLE go to crazy extremes. Some even try to combine two great loves, like the man who attempted to raise $2.5 million to buy a thirty-second commercial spot during the 2007 Super Bowl so he could propose to his girlfriend of five years. Although he got as far as filming the ad, no sponsors were willing to give up what is the most lucrative airtime on American television.

What would you be willing to do for love's sake? The Father's love for you and me was so powerful that he sent Jesus to the world. John 3:16 tells us, "For God so loved the world that He gave His only begotten Son, that whoever believes in Him should not perish but have everlasting life." Now that is what I call love.

The cause of Christ is, in fact, encapsulated in that one statement, "that whoever believes in Him should not perish but have everlasting life." Jesus is humanity's bridge to God the Father and eternity. He came to find you and connect you to the hope, the future, and the eternal plan the King has for you.

But if God's goal was simply about you believing in him, you would think he would take you straight to heaven as soon as you commit your life to him; say the salvation prayer and *whoosh*, off to heaven you go. But no, the Lord leaves us down here on earth, and with good reason. We believers become his hands and feet here on the planet, and our part in his eternal plan is both significant and a great honor.

You, as part of the body of Christ that extends all around the world, are commissioned by Jesus to become a fisher of men (Matt. 4:19). We, as God's church, become a great net of salvation, bringing answers, hope, and love to those who are yet to believe in him.

Jesus gave his disciples a great commission just before he was arrested by the Pharisees and sentenced to death:

All authority has been given to Me in heaven and on earth. Go therefore and make disciples of all the nations, baptizing them in the name of the Father and of the Son and of the Holy Spirit, teaching them to observe all things that I have commanded you; and lo, I am with you always, even to the end of the age. (Matt. 28:18–20)

Ultimately you and I are products of the first disciples' obedience to that command, just as future generations of believers will be the result of our obedience to that same commission.

You are here to exemplify Jesus to the world, and your testimony, conviction, and commitment to the cause of Christ is about ushering people into relationship with a God who loves them.

> *The church — including you and me — is the beacon . . . God uses to illuminate the earth.*

The Greek word for church, *ecclesia*, means "the called out ones." You have been chosen and called out by the Lord, not to be removed from the world, but to be light to a world that has yet to believe.

Jesus tells us to make our light shine "that they may see your good works and glorify your Father in heaven" (Matt. 5:16).

He is the light, but the church—including you and me— is the beacon, the lightbulb, he uses to illuminate the earth. A life lived for the cause of Christ shines intensely and, like a moth to the flame, it attracts people to God who lives in you.

Dead Religion

On a trip to Germany, I visited one of Munich's famous cathedrals. What I remember most about it is a box in the wall that contains a skeleton. In other cathedrals I have visited, the tombstones of believers from centuries gone by are cemented to the walls and floor, and tourists come in and out with cameras in hand, taking photos of the intricate stained glass. These churches, as beautiful as they are, have become tourist attractions admired more for their architecture than for the presence of God and his people.

This is contrary to the Father's plan for his church. He has called the church to be a powerful influence in our world. It is the Lord's will that the body of Christ be a dynamic living organism that produces life and affects lives.

Jesus was born for the cause, and the church is God's plan for implementing his cause—a cause that is empowered by three dynamic factors: (1) Jesus Christ, (2) the Holy Spirit, and (3) the church.

It is tragic that the church has at times lost sight of the cause of Christ. Form and ritual have sometimes crept in, replacing the freedom to worship Jesus Christ in spirit and in truth. The sad reality is that if we take Jesus Christ and the Holy Spirit out of the church equation, churches become ineffective and irrelevant.

In our changing society, church growth experts have noted that certain sectors of the church are declining. I believe churchgoers today do not want form; they want substance and authenticity. They want to express themselves in worship and receive Bible-based teaching that can be applied to their everyday lives. Church research in Australia also reveals that believers want to *be* the church, not just *go* to church. In other words, they want their faith to be channeled into making a positive difference to others.

It is no coincidence then that churches that are truly exalting Jesus Christ and bringing the power of the gospel to people in a relatable way are increasing and growing. I often say that it does not matter what denominational name is over the door of a church, as long as the name of Jesus is being proclaimed and the truth of his Word is being heard. Only the name of Jesus brings answers, freedom, and true fulfillment to people.

The Cause and the Church

I am passionate about the local church. I have been involved in church life my whole life, a fact I would not change for anything in the world. I love what I do, especially the amazing privilege of being a part of what Jesus said he would do, that is, building his church.

Jesus said, "I will *build my church;* and the gates of hell shall not prevail against it" (Matt. 16:18 KJV, emphasis added).

The gates of hell may try and keep people from a relationship with the Father, but Jesus promised that they would not prevail. On the cross Jesus unlocked and released us all from the prison that was death and gave us the promise of eternal life, but it is his church that connects people with this promise today. When the church is being the church, passionate about the cause of Christ and committed to seeing his kingdom take ground, we are, in fact, shining God's light (truth, hope, and power) into what is otherwise a pretty dark world.

Sadly, there are some who say they love God but dislike the church. In doing so, they despise the very thing Jesus loves and is committed to building. Then there are those who would try to convince the world that the church of Christ is fading into insignificance. The truth is the church is alive and taking ground. In 1900 there were approximately 558 million Christians in the world. At the beginning of the 21st century, Christians accounted for 33 percent of the world's population, or 2.1 billion people. It is pretty astounding when you think back two thousand or so years to the time when Jesus picked twelve unlikely candidates to be his disciples.

At Hillsong we are committed to championing the cause of the local church. To that end, all we do—from our conferences to the music we write—is underpinned by our immovable belief that it is through local churches of all shapes, sizes, and denominations that God changes people's lives and makes a difference in our communities.

For more than two decades, we have walked with those battling life-threatening illnesses, failing marriages, and the loss of beloved children. We have seen the isolated find a loving church community. We have celebrated successes with those who have overcome addictions or found the courage to tackle the pain of the past. We have applauded as young people passed exams, completed university, or secured their first jobs. We have celebrated engagements, weddings, births, anniversaries, and birthdays, and have seen lives lifted.

The church is not meant to be commandeered by the agendas of man or to be a place of manipulation, control, or greed.

The church is not about buildings or structures, nor should it be out of touch with real people and their real lives. The church is all about people, a loving family willing to extend the grace and love of Jesus Christ to humans, wherever they are along the journey.

The church is not meant to be commandeered by the agendas of man or to be a place of manipulation, control, or greed. It should also be more than just a nice place for Christians to meet on a Sunday. It is a community of people who love what the Lord loves—his church and people. It should be alive, active, and committed to connecting unbelievers with Jesus.

The Power of Being Planted

Being planted in a local church has brought incredible blessings into my life and that of my family. I have also seen the positive impact that the church has had on the lives of individuals, families, the young and not so young, the lonely, and those facing struggles.

Some of my favorite verses are Psalm 92:12–14 in *The Amplified Bible*:

The [uncompromisingly] righteous shall flourish like the palm tree [be long-lived, stately, upright, useful, and fruitful]; they shall grow like a cedar in Lebanon [majestic, stable, durable, and incorruptible]. *Planted in the house of the Lord, they shall flourish in the courts of our God.* [Growing in grace] they shall still bring forth fruit in old age; they shall be full of sap [of spiritual vitality] and [rich in the] verdure [of trust, love, and contentment]. (emphasis added)

We should all aspire to be "old saps," full of vitality and abounding in grace, trust, love, and contentment. When you are planted in the house of God, which is different from being a casual attendee, you are tapped in to receiving all the nourishment you need for your faith and life to grow strong and bear fruit.

I want to build the kind of church that releases people into their God-given potential.

This Scripture also puts an incredible responsibility and challenge on me as a church leader. If it is the will of the Father that people would flourish, I have to ask, "Can people flourish under my leadership? If they cannot flourish, why would people stay planted?"

As a pastor, I am not here to build a church simply to support my ministry or vision; I want to build the kind of church that releases people into their God-given potential. I need to ensure that the vision we are pursuing as a church is God-ordained and that it gives room for people to grow and for their dreams and hearts' desires to be established.

Linking your life, vision, and purpose to God's church will transform your life and will enable you to bring effectual and eternal change to the lives of others. You are a vital part of the body of Christ—His Church. It is the vehicle through which the kingdom of God takes ground and your life moves forward.

Your faith in Christ and your resources knitted together with mine and those of other believers gives us a truly wonderful opportunity to bring answers to a hurting world.

THE CAUSE
AND VISION

Chapter 3

Your Vision, His Cause

I VIVIDLY REMEMBER TWO YOUNG MEN, EACH with specific dreams and goals for the future, separately sharing with me their personal visions for their lives. Both had the potential and the initial track records for very real success in the business world.

The first enthused about his vision. "Brian, my ambition is to be a millionaire by the age of thirty!" He had set a goal for himself, and he certainly had the determination and potential to achieve it. But sadly, this young would-be entrepreneur, though full of vision then, today is nowhere to be seen. Inevitably, tough times struck, and vision alone was not enough to sustain him. Now well into his thirties, his vision remains unrealized.

The vision of the second young man, while sounding even more grandiose, impressed me more. "Brian," he said, "my personal vision is to help fund the salvation of the earth." To him, business was a tool with which to accomplish great things for the cause of the King and the kingdom. He, too, has faced difficult moments through the years, but he has held tight to his vision and has never lost his way.

It is great to have goals and ambitions in life, but the fact that the second man's vision was linked to a cause gave it power, sustainability, and much greater impetus. A vision without a cause is little more than a set of personal goals. Conversely, a vision attached to a cause is decidedly more than a hit-and-miss affair. If you live for a greater purpose or cause, you are on track to live the life of an overcomer and fulfill your God-given destiny.

> *A vision without a cause is little more than a set of personal goals.*

Vision Tied to a Cause

A lot has been said and written about vision over the years, and there is no doubt that vision gives direction and purpose.

I personally love spending time with and reading about visionary leaders. They challenge and inspire me. Focusing on the vision of others is rather like iron sharpening iron, stirring up creativity and innovative ideas, encouraging me to keep pressing on toward the dreams in my heart for our own lives, for Hillsong Church, and every person and family impacted by its ministries and outreaches.

Proverbs 29:18 tells us that without vision people live carelessly. They lack direction, conviction, and commitment. On the other hand, a life imbued by vision is one that is moving forward and on course with destiny.

A life imbued by vision is one that is moving forward and on course with destiny.

In Habakkuk 2:2 the Lord told Habakkuk, "Write the vision and make it plain on tablets, that he may run who reads it."

A defined vision gives us both a reason to run and something worth running after. A lot of people have vision, and they are ready to run with their vision, but they cannot get off the starting blocks. What makes the difference? Well, any vision is only as effective as the cause to which it is attached.

Vision should flow out of our unfolding revelation of Christ and his cause. Without this progressive revelation,

Proverbs 29:18 tells us that "the people perish" (KJV).

Christ's cause will empower your vision and give you the legs to run. When you direct your motivation, thinking, talent, time, and relationships toward the cause of the King, the principle of cause and effect is activated. Everything you put your hand to has greater effect and in turn is a catalyst for other things.

My life's vision has been fueled and empowered by my commitment to the cause of Christ. My own determination and ability could only have taken me so far, and clearly the grace of God has resulted in my pastoring a church that has influence and opportunity that vision alone could not produce.

I could write about many areas of our church, but the best known would be Hillsong's praise and worship. Over the years our music has been accredited with more than thirty gold and platinum sales awards worldwide and is distributed in some eighty nations. In recent years a new generation of musicians and songwriters has emerged out of our youth ministry. Their powerful and heartfelt praise and worship have connected with people in our church and all around the world.

I am often asked why our music has gone so far. Certainly, I aspired to lead a church that would write and record worship that testified to the greatness of an almighty God, but the success of our music cannot be attributed to vision alone. The key to understanding the prolonged favor on Hillsong's music lies much deeper. Our church has been gripped by the cause of Christ and his church. Our songwriters, worship leaders, musicians, and congregation are consumed with the idea of serving the cause of the King and the kingdom. Long before these songs make it onto an album, they are sung in our church services as praise and worship to the Lord. They are all about ushering people into the presence of God and bringing glory to him.

When your vision is tied to the cause of Christ, there is a power and momentum to all you do. While vision is fantastic, the cause has even greater significance than your vision.

A Vision Is Something You Possess, But the Cause Possesses You

Jesus was captivated and consumed by his Father's cause. It affected and directed every aspect of his life. It was not something he held in his own hand or a possession he could hold or let go; rather, he was in its hand. The cause of his Father possessed him. Not persecution, pain, religious opposition, or any alternatives or options could dissuade him.

Even in the face of death, Jesus was able to pray, "My Father, if this cup cannot pass away from Me unless I drink it, Your will be done" (Matt. 26:42). Jesus was gripped by a cause.

In the same way, when you are committed to the Father's

cause, you do not have to make up a vision for your life. It takes hold of you and begins to influence everything you do. Your life begins to be lived in a way that honors the Father and is about seeing his kingdom extended.

The cause of Christ holds you in its hand, giving each day direction, purpose, and an eternal perspective. It puts a fire in your belly and gives you the tenacity to face challenges head-on and the willingness to do whatever it takes.

I have more to say about purpose in the chapters to come, but undoubtedly any man or woman with a sense of a cause that possesses him or her has a huge advantage in life. Purpose and vision are an endless flow, and when you understand this, you begin approaching life as the apostle

The cause of Christ . . . puts a fire in your belly and gives you the tenacity to face challenges head-on and the willingness to do whatever it takes.

Paul did. You forget that which is behind and reach forward to what is ahead. You "press toward the goal for the prize of the upward call of God in Christ Jesus" (Phil. 3:14). Does the cause possess you, or are you trying to stay motivated by a vision you possess?

A Vision Can Be Personal,
But a Cause Is Bigger Than Any One Person

Perhaps vision is not your problem. You know the direction you want your life to take and can talk about it with great excitement and enthusiasm. Maybe you have your personal vision statement with one-year, five-year, and ten-year goals, but whom does your vision serve? Vision alone can exist for our own purposes and interests, whereas a cause extends well beyond us. It is bigger than any individual or organization. I have my personal vision, and our church has a very specific vision with an accompanying vision statement:

> To reach and influence the world by building a large, *Christ-centered*, Bible-based church; changing mind-sets and empowering people to lead and impact in every sphere of life.

Our vision statement is clear, succinct, and defines what we want to accomplish and who we want to reach. But so what? There is no power if it is all about us and our vision. The cause of Christ is not our own domain. It is a cause greater than any one individual, ministry, mission, or church.

Naturally, I am delighted when people understand and catch the vision of our church, but as a church leader, I know that the cause of God is far more powerful in the hearts of a congregation than commitment to a vision. If our church has Christ's cause in its spirit and our vision reflects and serves that cause, people will want to partner in our vision. Furthermore, their own lives will overflow with personal vision because they are aligned and inspired by a much greater cause.

The beauty of the cause of Christ: we all have a part to play. There is room for different visions and mission statements, but the cause embraces them all.

> *The cause of Christ is not our own domain.*

Imagine politicians, entrepreneurs, artists, professionals, ministries, and homes all filled with a personal vision fueled by a greater cause. Vision is critical, but of even greater value is the cause. *Is your vision bigger than you are?*

A Vision Can Exist for You, but You Exist for the Cause

During one of my ministry trips, the youth leader of the church where I was to minister picked me up from the airport. I asked him about his work, and he began to tell me how frustrated he was because the pastor of the church would not get behind his vision for the youth ministry. My reply to him was, "It isn't your pastor's job to get behind your vision. It is your job to work out what the vision of the church is and serve that vision through the youth ministry."

His mistake was in thinking that his church existed for him and his vision, when in fact, he existed to fulfill the cause of Christ and serve it through the vision of his church. He had developed the thinking that the church existed for him.

Many people fall into the same trap. I remember hearing the story of a young doctor who was on the fast track to promotion. He had studied hard and made the honors list and soon held a lucrative position in a well-known hospital. He had always dreamed that medicine would bring him lots of money, vast opportunities, and a lavish lifestyle. At that point in life, his dream seemed to be coming true. Then one day, while flipping through a medical journal, he read an article about the impact that AIDS was having on children in Africa, and his heart was moved. He soon realized that a vision could encompass more than just his own plans. Moved by compassion, he committed himself to using his skills and his abilities to help in a cause greater than his own. He has since worked on short-term medical teams and assisted in training African doctors to help them provide health care and support to those in desperate need. He realized his vision did not exist just for him; it existed for a greater purpose.

When the purpose of your vision is not so much about you but is for the sake of something much bigger, you discover the *power* of the cause. This involves living a life well beyond yourself.

I am amazed at how much enthusiasm and commitment are injected into church ministry when people get a revelation of how they can help outwork God's cause through their lives and through the church.

Those who are sick do not merely receive their healing for themselves, but so that they can be effective for the kingdom. Businesspeople who prosper financially are not blessed for the sole purpose of storing up wealth for themselves; their resources enable them to help others in a far greater capacity than had they not prospered. "Each part [of the body] gets its meaning from the body as a whole, not the other way around" (Rom. 12:4 MSG). When we are cause-centered, we exist for the sake of the cause of Christ. *Does your vision exist to serve the cause?*

You Would Not Die for a Vision, But Jesus Died for the Cause

In the days following the demise of the Soviet Union, the attention of the world media was drawn to the little town of Groznyy, where a small group of Chechnyan rebels made a stand against the might of the Russian army. They were not fighting for a vision; they were fighting to the death for their cause. Similarly, suicide bombers have chosen to give their lives for the sake of their cause. Sadly, this is an ugly perversion in which vision has been devastatingly misdirected and misguided. The illustration of suicide bombers does, however, reinforce an important point: people will not die for someone else's vision, but many choose to die for a cause, no matter how violent or wrong it might be.

It was not vision that nailed Jesus to the cross; it was the cause of his Father. Jesus predicted his death on the cross, saying, "For this cause came I unto this hour" (John 12:27 KJV).

Jesus made the ultimate sacrifice—his life—for the cause. It is unlikely you and I will ever face the possibility of being martyred for the gospel's sake, unlike thousands of Christians around the world each year who die in the name of Jesus. But are you willing to let your vision die for the cause of Christ?

You may have a fantastic vision for your life, and there may be those who get excited about their own personal visions, but how many would willingly surrender their lives for those visions?

> *Jesus made the ultimate sacrifice—his life—for the cause.*

I am astounded at how willingly those who have a revelation of the King and the kingdom will lay down their lives for the sake of Christ's cause. They commit their time, their finances, and their energy to serve him. They readily realign their personal vision to serve a bigger cause and become so much more fulfilled because of it. *Is your vision worth dying for?*

A Vision Gives You a Way Out, But the Cause Leaves You No Options

As a church pastor, I do not have a normal weekend the way other people do. Hillsong Church has two major worship centers, located forty minutes apart. With multiple services on each of these campuses and fourteen extension services at other locations, there is a lot for me to do on any given weekend. Obviously, the leisure of reading the Sunday newspapers over a cappuccino at a beachside café or the smell of a freshly mown lawn is not a part of my usual Sunday routine. Sunday nights are never about football or fireside chats, but I never feel as though I am missing out, because I am doing what I was born to do.

As a teenager, I remember being invited to a Sunday afternoon beach barbecue, but I had a commitment at church for an extra meeting. I was not happy to be the odd man out as all my friends were heading for the beach, but that day became pivotal in my life. I realized that the vision God had placed in my heart to pursue his call on my life would mean that Sundays would never be my own. The cause of the King meant I had to die to all other options.

The apostle Paul spoke of how the love of God compelled

him (2 Cor. 5:14). In other words, the love of God left him with no other choice. When your life is gripped by a cause, the alternatives disappear. When Jesus told his disciples about his death, he knew there was no other way:

> Now My soul is troubled, and what shall I say? "Father, save Me from this hour"? But for this purpose I came to this hour. (John 12:27)

There was no option for Jesus but to be nailed to the cross. It is what he came to earth for. He died that the perfect will of the Father might be done through his life.

Compare this to Carol, a gifted young woman, who seemed to have an abundance of opportunities at her feet upon completing school. She considered law, engineering, architecture, economics, and a range of other options. People told her that law was a great career choice for her, and she could see herself one day becoming a Supreme Court judge. Unsure of what path to take, Carol enrolled in law, but six months into her studies, her interest waned. She kept second-guessing her decision to become a lawyer. Lacking motivation and short of cash, she quit college and has since tried a plethora of odd jobs, vowing to one day complete her studies.

When vision is detached from a cause, people can start to think that the grass is greener somewhere else. Vision without a cause has options. If things become discouraging, you can put the causeless vision aside or change direction. You can choose to run with a vision, or you can choose to abandon it. You hold a vision in your hand, but a cause grips your heart. It will not let you go, even in life's most discouraging moments. *Does your vision leave you with options?*

> *You hold a vision in your hand, but a cause grips your heart.*

A Vision Can Be Ignored, But You Cannot Ignore the Cause

When Bobbie and I were first married, I was a youth pastor in a small suburban church and worked as a sales representative for a multinational company. When I started at the company, they gave me a huge manual that contained information about the organization, its founder, and its mission statement. I was expected to read it and know their vision. I gave my best in the time I worked there (and I appreciated the company car and salary), but I must confess that I already had a vision for my life. My dreams and aspirations were linked to the cause of Christ, making it difficult to get inspired by the history and vision of my employers.

On a daily basis you may drive past all sorts of small busi-

nesses, large corporations, clubs, or various other organiza-
tions, but it is unlikely that you take much time to ponder
their individual mission or vision statements. That is because
someone else's vision is often easy to ignore. But you cannot
ignore a cause.

When Martin Luther King Jr. spoke about equality for
African-Americans or Nelson Mandela pursued with total
abandon an end to apartheid in South Africa, there was no
ignoring the causes that drove them. Today, years after the
respective visions of these two great men were first conceived,
the causes to which they committed their lives are known by
people all over the world and continue to be taught to new
generations. *Is your vision easy to ignore?*

A Vision Will Generate Excitement, But the Cause Generates Power

During the three years of Jesus' ministry, excited crowds
gathered wherever he went. "Could this be the Messiah?" they
asked. "How can he perform such miracles?" others exclaimed.
The crowds were excited about the possibility that Jesus
was the promised Savior. Others simply came to join in the
spectacle. But when the crunch came, many in the crowd
deserted him, calling instead for his crucifixion.

Compare this to the apostles and the other disciples who
understood the cause for which Jesus came to earth. Granted,

a few of them faltered when they saw Jesus hanging on the cross, but when they realized he had risen as promised, they were filled with power.

They lived for his cause and performed great exploits and miracles in the name of Jesus. They gave sight to the blind, healed the sick, and overcame great challenges and persecution because they had been empowered by the Holy Spirit.

When Bobbie and I were newly married, we decided to move to Australia from New Zealand to be part of what was then my dad's church, Sydney Christian Life Centre. (Many years later it became part of what is now Hillsong Church.) We were full of vision and excited about what the future might hold. Then we landed. We were living in a little apartment, and Bobbie and I had to work hard to make ends meet. She worked as a secretary. In addition to serving in the church, I had a number of different jobs, including one as a window cleaner. Looking at it naturally, the vision we had before heading to Australia seemed a long way off. If vision had been the only thing that was keeping us there, the excitement easily could have waned, and we might have been tempted to catch the next plane home. But we were fueled by something much deeper than ourselves. We were passionate about the greater cause, and we were expectant, hungry, and committed to paying whatever price to see the power of God impact our lives and the lives of others. The apostle Paul wrote: "I am not ashamed of the gospel of Christ, for it is the *power* of God to salvation" (Rom. 1:16, emphasis added).

Vision generates excitement and enthusiasm, but the cause of Christ *generates power.* If you allow the Savior's cause to penetrate your life, it will *empower* your relationships, your plans for the future, and your connection to the world. *Is your vision a power generator?*

Author Helen Keller once said, "The only thing worse than being blind is having sight but no vision." Although I agree with the sentiment of this statement, I believe there is something even worse than having sight with no vision, and that is having a vision that is only self-focused and self-motivated.

On its own a vision has limitations, but when linked to the cause of Christ, it has supernatural power and purpose. When you surrender your vision and future into God's hands and align them with his will, your life is a miracle waiting to happen. The cause of Christ will take your personal vision, your passions, dreams, and goals to levels you could never have imagined.

Vision is essential, but the cause is powerful. The cause of the King is the impetus that keeps the church moving forward as a united force on the earth. Your vision tied to mine and that of other believers and underpinned by the cause brings great power and momentum. Together we have an incredible opportunity to bring positive and eternal change.

Chapter 4

United Around the Cause

THE DAY TWO PEOPLE GET MARRIED IS THE start of a powerful partnership for the cause of Christ. Sadly, over the years, Bobbie and I have been forced to watch as the once-happy marriages of some of our friends have broken down, ending in acrimonious divorces. It is tough to watch, and ultimately it is a losing situation for everyone.

Some 80 percent of divorces are granted on the basis of irreconcilable differences. These differences may be due to infidelity, a lack of communication, or a multitude of other reasons, but often the differences are grounded in the fact that the vision that each partner had for their marriage, their family, and their future diverged. The result? Vision became division, and where there was once unity, there was now disunity.

In Matthew 12:25, when the Pharisees accused Jesus of casting out demons by Beelzebub (the prince of demons), he responded, "Every kingdom divided against itself is brought to desolation, and every city or house divided against itself will not stand."

Jesus here talks about a kingdom, a city, and a house. The point, as it applies to our lives today, is that just as division can bring down a nation (think coup), it can and will ultimately destroy a church, a marriage, or an individual life.

A house full of division is not a pleasant place to be. When we think of division, we tend to think of strife, anger, fighting, and people splitting away.

Division in a church is a little like division in a marriage. When the church is functioning the way God intends, it can be heaven. When it is not, it can be hell.

A house divided does not necessarily mean that people are fighting and punching each other around the communion table, or that a husband and wife are pitching plates and vases at each other. A divided house is one that is going in different directions. If we are truly one, we need to be going in a single direction.

The Pharisees were often divided among themselves. John 7:43 and John 9 speak of this division. Legalism and bondage lend themselves to division. But in a house (be it a church or a home) where people are empowered, released, and have a sense of vision and leadership that inspires, people will flourish.

A single vision united around a cause, be it in a church, a marriage, a family, or a workplace, will help guard against division.

A House Divided Has Divided Motives

When motives are pure, the house of God is awesome. There is a huge difference between people who use their vision to build the house of God and people who use the house of God to build their vision. When people's motives are to use the house of God in a negative way, division is inevitable.

I never want to be a controlling leader, but I do need to understand and be a discerner

> *When people's motives are to use the house of God in a negative way, division is inevitable.*

of people's hearts. Failure to do so would put our church at risk and thwart our ability to serve the cause and the kingdom of God effectively.

Take, for example, a businessperson who is using his or her

gifts and connections to be a blessing to the house of God. This is completely different from those who come into the house of God thinking about how people in the church can help them build their businesses.

As Hillsong's profile has gained recognition, people have come who have tried to utilize the leverage of our church's name by attaching it to their business or ministry. You would be astounded at how creative some people can be. We have become well versed in discerning wrong motives. It is similar to what happened when I was growing up. I was treated differently at school and in the community when people found out that my dad was a prominent pastor in our part of the world.

When your motives are genuinely driven to serve the Lord's purposes, God will see that his house and your life flourish, but when motives are going in different directions, the house divides.

A House Divided Has Divided Vision

I often tell our church that we have one vision that is outworked in many different ways. Imagine how complicated and confusing, not to mention divisive, it would be if every one of our departments had a different vision.

We would experience utter chaos. There would be no cohesion, and in time, splinter groups would form and go their separate ways. Division in the case of a church will minimize that church's impact, but division will also negatively affect the people of that church as they are pulled to and fro, unsure whose vision to follow and what cause they are contributing to.

The same can be said of a family or a business partnership in which one spouse or partner is pursuing one vision, while the other is going in a completely different direction. The children or employees in that family or business are put in a very difficult situation, and in time, irreconcilable differences will arise.

When your house, family, marriage, friendships, business, and church have a united vision and a focus anchored on a greater cause, there is a great sense of stability and security because everyone knows where he or she is heading, and people have something to follow.

A House Divided Has Divided Loyalties

Jesus had a disloyal friend named Judas whose divided loyalty caused him to betray Jesus for thirty pieces of silver. He is the type of friend Proverbs 18:24 describes this way: "The man of many friends [a friend of all the world] will prove himself a bad friend" (AMP, brackets in original).

Proverbs 18:24 is saying that people who try to be loyal to everyone actually are not good friends to anyone. Judas tried to be both a friend to Jesus and to the Pharisees, but he failed at both and ended up hanging himself.

I am reminded of people who come to church on Sunday and lift their hands in worship, but during the week live like hell. Sadly, in time, this kind of divided loyalty will lead to destruction.

God values loyalty, and undivided loyalty is an important characteristic for all of us. Strength comes when you know where your loyalties lie. Loyalty actually forces you to take sides.

No doubt you have heard of an "us-and-them" spirit. It is one I do not let fester in our church. I ask our leaders, "On which side of 'us and them' do you find yourselves?" Loyalty always positions itself as one of "them." You can build the church, a marriage, and friendships on that kind of loyalty.

There will be times when you will have to make a stand about where your loyalties lie, particularly when it comes to the house of God. It is impossible to be a friend to the house of God and a friend to the world simultaneously.

Living for the Father's cause is about making the tough decisions in life. This includes with whom and what you are "friends." You need to position yourself to be best friends with God's house, guarding against division and determining in your heart that nothing will draw you away from building his kingdom.

A House Divided Has Diminished Capacity

There are lots of great causes in the world to pursue, but if you try to tackle them all, you will not get very far. As a unified group, Christians can have greater impact, particularly in terms of resources and ministry, than an individual can alone.

Imagine if you landed in a war-torn country with one bag of rice but with a goal of feeding all the hungry and destitute. Your rice would not go very far. However, if you combined your effort and resources with those of others, your effectiveness would be far greater. Simply put, your contribution, your vision, linked to a united effort can make a much bigger difference.

This is a principle we read about in Malachi. The Lord says, "Bring all the tithes into the storehouse, that there may be food in My house" (Mal. 3:10). When accompanied by clear vision and strategy, a full storehouse enables us to have a greater impact.

Conversely, division weakens the greater whole, and our ability to meet people's needs,

There is something very powerful in a force of people unified in action and in response.

bring answers, and take the gospel of Christ to the world is diminished.

The Bible talks of two being better than one because they have good reward for their labor (Eccl. 4:9), and the same is true when it comes to the vision and cause to which we are committed. There is something very powerful in a force of people unified in action and in response.

United We Stand

Many, many years ago, I faced what perhaps was my most embarrassing experience. I went to preach in a little town in Australia and was staying in the home of someone from the church. They had placed a guest towel on my bed, and you know what it can be like staying in someone else's home—a little uncomfortable—so I thought I would try and get to the shower early to avoid spoiling anyone's routine. With church clothes in hand, I headed to the bathroom. Only after getting out of the shower did I realize to my dismay that the lovely clean towel was still sitting on the edge of my bed! There was little choice; I had to make a run for it. Poking my head out of the door, I found the corridor empty and the house silent. I started my dash. I had only gone a few steps when to my horror the door handle of the room next to mine began to turn. I had to make a split-second decision: did I make a run for my room or try and make it back to the sanctuary of the bathroom? My decision proved fatal. As I turned to try and make it back to the bathroom, I lost my footing on the now-wet corridor and fell with a crash! Wisely, whoever was behind that door shut it. To this day, I do not know who opened the door or just how much he or she saw. But I can say that breakfast was awfully quiet!

When you attempt to go in two different directions—whether the tug-of-war is between pursuing God's purposes for your life and worldly pursuits or between a core business concept and new business pursuits or between two friends whose interests and direction have diverged—there is inevitably going to be some kind of major division or break; things are going to snap.

If we are truly one, and if we are truly to be united, then we need to be going in a single direction. A kingdom divided against itself cannot stand (Mark 3:24). Wherever there is division, wrong motives, disloyalty, and disunity, the purposes of God cannot stand.

When it comes to your vision, your time, your giving, and your support, I encourage you to unite with a church and with people who are single-minded in their vision to serve the Lord and his church.

Chapter 5

An Eternal Vision

AT THE TURN OF THE MILLENNIUM, THE NEW Year celebrations in the city of Sydney, Australia, were broadcast to a TV audience estimated at three billion people. The countdown from 1999 to 2000 triggered one of the greatest fireworks displays the city had ever seen, illuminating the city skyline, the Sydney Opera House, and the Harbour Bridge. At the climax of the spectacular finale, a single word emblazoned the bridge in fifty-foot-high neon letters: "Eternity."

What a significant and powerful message for every human being across the face of the earth—the contemplation of eternity.

The story behind the use of the word *eternity* commemorates the life of a man who died in 1967 at the age of eighty-three. Arthur Stace was not a history-making politician, nor was he a world-class athlete. He had virtually no education and from the age of fifteen, his criminal activities led to a succession of jail sentences. During the years of the Great Depression, he lived on handouts and slid further down the road to alcoholism. Yet the story of his life is told all over the world today because of one single word that impacted his life: *eternity*.

In 1930 Arthur Stace found himself in a local church service, and his encounter with God changed his life forever. It was the word *eternity* that stuck in his mind and, taking a piece of chalk from his pocket, he felt compelled to write it on the pavement. For one who could hardly write his own name, he found he could write "eternity" quite elegantly.

For the next thirty-seven years, Arthur Stace would wake up early, and after an hour's prayer, he would write his word in chalk on the sidewalks of Sydney. Over the years, that one-word sermon became the object of much public speculation and curiosity as many contemplated its meaning.

Although a number of decades have passed since Arthur Stace died, the evangelistic message of *eternity* continues to live on, capturing the attention of another generation.

Eternity. It is what we are saved for, and as Arthur Stace demonstrated, it is this message that we are called to take to others. Although you may not use chalk to communicate your message, everything about you—what you live for, how you live your life, and, your confession—can provoke people to think about eternity.

I am inspired by the story of an old Australian preacher and pioneer. Not one to settle for retirement, he was still preaching the Word well into his eighties. During one Sunday service, he had just finished preaching his sermon, and the congregation began to sing, "Within the veil I now would come, / into your Holy Place to look upon Thy face." [1] And he did! He went to eternity right in the middle of worship.

> *Everything about you—what you live for, how you live your life, and, your confession—can provoke people to think about eternity.*

That preacher had a vision of eternity not only for himself, but he was leading and saving people from a Christless eternity right up to his last breath. What a way to go!

Empowering the Generations

Not only is the Lord the greatest of visionaries (He created the world—the sun, the moon, the sky, the seas—and everything on it with no blueprints or architectural drawings), he is also generational. When God called Abraham to leave his hometown of Ur, God had future generations in mind. The lineage of Abraham extended right through to Jesus. When the Father sent Jesus to die on the cross, he did so for the sake of the generations to come. The reason we are on the planet today is to leave a legacy for future generations to build on.

We all are on loan to this world, and while here, we are simply stewards of the vision God has given us. One day a new generation will take over where we leave off, and I pray they will pursue with even greater fervor the things of God.

Bobbie and I are deliberate in our efforts to equip and release the younger generations in the outworking of our church's vision. The young people of today have increased skills and strengths, and I pray that my vision will be too small for them.

We all need to be committed to empowering future generations to do even greater exploits in God's name than we have done and to believe that the Lord will give them vision for things we could never imagine.

My hope and prayer is that as the coming generations

look back in history to the twenty-first century, they will marvel at the power of God, the progress of the church, and the advancement of the kingdom. I believe we have a responsibility to the legend and legacy we will leave to those who come after us.

Put simply, your vision is not just for you; it is for those to come. It is of eternal consequence. We all live in the tension between birth and death, and although I do not know when God will call you home, I do know that he wants us to live with an eternal perspective that embraces the generations.

Your life can impact the future. How do you want future generations to remember you?

Your life can impact the future. How do you want future generations to remember you? Buildings and land may outlast us and our visions, but the cause of the King and the kingdom will continue into eternity.

THE CAUSE
AND CALLING

Chapter 6

Saved and Called

WHEN I WAS A TEENAGER, THERE WAS ALWAYS great excitement when the end-times preacher was coming to town. His arrival seemed to be one surefire way to guarantee a packed house. I must say it appeared very unlikely in that 1970s environment that we would still be here in the twenty-first century. Much speculation centered on the United Nations, the European Economic Community, and on who was shaping up to be the likely Antichrist.

Novels about Armageddon and the end of the world still make the *New York Times* best seller lists, and issues of eternity rightly demand our attention, but in hindsight, so much of the focus when I was growing up seemed to be on the here-after instead of the here and now.

I believe two things are certain: first, Jesus is coming again, and second, we are "saved" for reasons that extend beyond our own eternal security.

There is no greater joy than to see people surrender their lives to Christ, and each weekend at Hillsong Church many people respond to the life-transforming message of Jesus. Jesus died on the cross and rose again to give humanity the opportunity to be saved. Using the analogy of a person caught in swelling seas and a dangerous riptide, he or she would surely perish without intervention from a rescuer. However, with the help of a rescue team of people who put their lives on the line to save others, the swimmer caught in the riptide is pulled out of the life-threatening situation and brought out of harm's way. That is exactly what Jesus does for us at our point of salvation. He pulls us out of sin and death into the safety of a new life with him.

Saved! What a miraculous provision that is, but salvation is not one-dimensional. It is much more than raising a hand and praying a salvation prayer. Furthermore, it is not only about the afterlife. Millions of Christ's followers have experienced the joy of salvation, but I have a vital question for you. Are you simply living as one who is *saved*, or have you taken up the challenge to live as one who is *called*? It is

important that we grasp the revelation
saved, but we are also *called* for a purp

Sandwiched between your salvation (o.
the Father) and God's grace (his favor, blessing, and
is your calling and purpose.

When the Lord saves you, he has much more than just
your eternity in mind. He has called you to make a difference
here on earth. Second Timothy 1:9 tells us that God "has
saved us and called us with a
holy calling, not according to
our works, but according to
His own purpose and grace
which was given to us in Christ
Jesus before time began."

> *Being saved is
> not just our
> superannuation
> plan for eternity.*

Again in 2 Thessalonians
2:13–14 we are told that we
have been chosen by the King
of kings, saved through the cross, and called that we might
share in the glory of Jesus. As Ecclesiastes 3:11 explains,
this calling is tied to things of eternal significance, or in
other words, the cause of Christ:

He also has planted eternity in men's hearts and minds [a
divinely implanted sense of a purpose working through the
ages which nothing under the sun but God alone can satisfy],

et so that men cannot find out what God has done from the beginning to the end. (AMP, brackets in original)

This divinely implanted sense of purpose adds another dimension to salvation. Being saved is not just our superannuation plan for eternity; it is an active and progressive fulfillment of God's purpose every day of our lives here on earth, which is intended not only to transform us, but also to reach others.

A Holy Calling

The weight and responsibility implied by the apostle Paul in his use of "holy calling" (2 Tim. 1:9) has caused some Christians to tie themselves in knots as they have tried to discover and seek out what a holy calling in fact looks like. Some have retreated to mountainous caves for undisturbed prayer and contemplation, while others have pursued fierce theological debates on the topic in an effort to find answers.

The truth is that our calling is not found in the ethereal; it is found in the here and now.

I find it difficult to reconcile the God I know and love, who so willingly sacrificed his Son, Jesus Christ, on a cross, with a

God who would make our calling so unattainable. The truth is that our calling is not found in the ethereal; it is found in the here and now.

We can sometimes put too much emphasis on trying to work out what this calling looks like. "Am I called to be a pastor or to start a business or pursue a career that will enable me to raise kingdom finances? Am I called to serve in the women's ministry and reach out to other mums or is my calling supposed to be outworked in the developing world?" I actually believe there are things in your heart that the Lord has deposited there, and as you begin to step out in faith, keeping God central, he will begin to reveal, refine, and release you in your holy calling.

As I will go on to explain, this calling encompasses all aspects of your life. It is not just lived out on Sunday at church or during midweek Bible study. It should be impacting your family, relationships, Mums at Mother's group, the person who works in the office next to yours, and the person who served you your morning coffee.

Simply put, every day, every conversation, every situation, every endeavor—your career, finances, relationships, each expression of your gifts and talents—are all an opportunity to be living out your holy calling.

Bobbie and I have been married for thirty years now, and perhaps the greatest strength of our marriage has been our united sense of calling and purpose. It has been wonderful to witness each of our adult children making the life-changing decision to follow Christ, but even more rewarding has been watching each of them count the cost and make the choices to fulfill their individual callings. It has been our experience that a marriage and family with a healthy understanding of the difference between simply living as *saved* children of God and deciding to live as *called* children of God will be a unified family. Our commitment as a family has been to use what the Lord has put in our hands to fulfill his purposes.

When Bobbie and I decided to get married all those years ago, central to our plans was our dream to one day build a great church. We agreed then that we were prepared to make whatever sacrifices were necessary to do something significant with our lives.

During our engagement, we spent hours excitedly talking about our future together. One particular occasion stands out in my memory. I was living in a rented house occupied by nine, single, young males, all part of our youth group at the time. The very thought of that house still causes me to relive all the associated smells and atmosphere of that experience!

Mrs. Wilson was the next-door neighbor, and on this particular night, Bobbie and I had parked at the top of her very steep driveway. So entranced and absorbed were we in our discussion about our dreams of what our future would hold that we failed to notice the hand brake was not on and the car was not in gear. We also were completely oblivious as the vehicle began to move and gather speed, hurtling toward Mrs. Wilson's house. Our trance was shockingly broken by the rousing crash of a splintering garage door—as was the slumber of Mrs. Wilson and the entire neighborhood—at 2:00 a.m.!

Those innocent yet God-ordained plans have consistently been a central part of our relationship, and a strong sense of calling has always played a key role in our life together. We always wanted to take every opportunity or open door God gave us to fulfill kingdom purpose.

Did we know all the finer details of how our calling would be outworked? No, we did not have a clue at that point. We did not think it would include moving to Australia or planting a church that would in time gather people from all over our city. What we did know, as we sat in the car that night talking about our dreams and vision for the future, is that God would always be at the center of our decisions and all that we did. We were committed to being obedient to his Word and direction. The rest was in his hands.

To live as one who is saved is to be connected to Jesus Christ, to live as one who is called is all about serving him, and "to be graced" relates to God's enabling or empowering. When you decide that your salvation is about God, and you combine that with your calling, he adds his grace to it, and suddenly you are on course with his purpose and destiny.

I pray that each of us would understand that we are saved and called for purposes much bigger than ourselves. Living as one who is saved but not called is a waste of what God intends for you.

Chapter 7

Use What Is in Your Hand

WHEN IT COMES TO COORDINATION, I WOULD say I am more than a little challenged, something my sons and anyone else who has ever played backyard football with me would no doubt attest to! However, this fact did not dampen my desire as a young boy to one day play for the All Blacks, New Zealand's international rugby team.

Quite clearly, though, the laws of physics have conspired against me, and it would seem that God did not call me to be a rugby star (if he had, he would have made my legs a little quicker), but he did call me to build his church and to be a pastor.

When I was a youth leader in a little church in New Zealand, I held a Thursday night home Bible study. It began to grow really fast, and soon it was almost larger than the Sunday morning church meeting. Building the church has come pretty naturally to me, and I believe God has graced and enabled me to do it. Although I would have struggled to make it on the football field, and in a lot of other areas, when I focused on those things that seemed like a natural fit and trusted the Lord to enable me to grow and learn, I began living in my purpose.

Today I have had the opportunity to see and do so many of the things that were in my heart to do when I was young. I could have pursued what was in my heart and totally missed my calling, but by focusing on what the Father had placed in my hand, many of the desires of my heart have come to pass.

Salvation is all about purpose, your calling is about purpose, and grace is about purpose. Remember, 2 Timothy 1:9 talks about being saved and called by Jesus for a holy calling he graces us for. The Lord has graced you for his purpose. Grace is God's enabling power, and by his grace he has given you gifts and talents to bring him glory.

I encourage you to think of your calling in terms of what God has put in your hand. Your calling includes your gifting, your talents, and the things you are good at. Think of purpose in terms of what God has put in your heart. Your purpose is what you love, what you are passionate about.

Whether you are good at the arts, mechanics, technology, speaking, or dancing, those things have been given to you for kingdom purpose. The reason we need to catch this concept of calling or purpose is that many people see what is in their hand as an obstacle to what he has put in their hearts. Human nature tends to underestimate what God's purposes might be. But everything comes back to bringing glory to God.

Colossians 1:17 says, "He is before all things, and in Him all things consist." In Him all things hold together—who you are, your health, your gifts, your time, your energy, your marriage, and your family. Life is all about God and his purposes. The best way to fulfill what the Lord has put in your heart is by being faithful with what he has put in your hand.

What Are You Holding?

What is in your hand? This is the question God asked of Moses in Exodus 4 as he was grappling with the fact that God had asked him to lead the people of Israel out of Egypt and the bondage they had lived in. Moses tried to convince the Lord that he was not the right person for the job. The gist of Moses' response to God recorded in Exodus 3 and 4 was, "Who am I and who is going to listen to me? How am I possibly going to do that?"

God replied, "What is that in your hand?" (Ex. 4:2).

Moses was holding a staff, and that is exactly what God told Moses to use in order to see God's desire to free the people of Israel fulfilled.

Often your calling is screaming at you; it is staring you in the face. It is what you do naturally, the very thing that is in your hand. Sometimes people are waiting for a still, small voice to tell them what their purpose and calling are. They tell God (and anyone in earshot), "I just don't know where I fit. I don't know what I'm supposed to do. I don't know what God's will is for my life." But the actual Bible word *called* means to "call out aloud." There is nothing still and small about it!

Ask yourself, "Where am I gifted? What are my talents? What comes naturally to me?" That is your calling.

There are those who say, "I just feel like God wants me to lay it down." The result can be Christian sportspeople who want to pastors, and pastors who want to be business-people, and worship leaders

> *We do not actually have the right to lay down or surrender what the Father has given to us as a gift.*

who want to be rock stars, and pastors who practically sing their sermons because they want to be worship leaders! The fact is that we do not actually have the right to lay down what the Father has given to us as a gift.

Maybe you have acquired some skills along the way that do not seem to have a whole lot to do with Jesus and the cause of Christ. Maybe over the years you acquired a knack for getting out of tricky situations by stretching the truth. If your gift is clearly at cross-purposes with God, then it is probably best to lay that talent down. But we can often underestimate the God-given gifts and talents we have.

James 1:17 says, "Every good gift and every perfect gift is from above, and comes down from the Father of lights." In other words, the Lord does not change his mind. He is not schizophrenic; he has not made you one way to use you a different way. God has given you gifts and talents for a purpose— his purpose.

I love telling the story about a friend of mine in England who pastored a church there. John had a billionaire (let's call him Paul) in his church, and I am talking British pounds! John tells of how one time Paul, the billionaire, came to him and said with tears in his eyes, "John, I would give anything to do what you do." And John said he looked straight back at him with tears in his eyes and said, "Paul, I'd give anything for you to be doing what I'm doing too!" What is it about us that wants to do what somebody else does?

There are a number of reasons why we attempt to pursue

what is in our hearts, rather than starting with what is in our hands. The first is:

What is in your hand often involves pressure, discipline, and diligence; what is in your heart is romantic. The pressure of the present is not on what is in your heart. Your heart holds a dream to which you can escape. Sometimes we get so enamored that we escape to the romance of what is in our hearts because the dreams of the heart do not feel like work; there is no pressure to achieve those dreams.

This escape to the dreams of the heart is similar to what happens on a bleak winter's day at work when you start to picture your summer holidays. You envision the sand, the sea, and just for a moment you get lost in the vision. The pressure of work, the children, and the mortgage disappears.

Genesis 8:22 tells us that as long as the earth endures, there will be a winter and a summer, so that summer holiday is real. It is coming, but the key is to keep doing what you are doing right now in this season.

What is in our hands is present and familiar; what is in our hearts is distant and mysterious. We often take for granted that which is familiar to us. Familiarity can cause us to fail to appreciate fully what we have in our hands. The Jews were looking for a Messiah, and Jesus, the Son of God, was actually among them. The Bible says the Jews were looking for a sign and the Greeks were looking for wisdom. But when Jesus was with them, the Jews thought of him as a stumbling block, and the Greeks saw him as foolishness (1 Cor. 1:23). The Israelites had created a mystery around the coming of the Messiah. They thought the Savior would be something akin to what we would describe as a great knight on a white horse, not a mere carpenter's son from Galilee. They were looking for the mysterious and missed what was right in front of them. We can do the same when it comes to what is in our hands. Do not underestimate the power of the things that flow naturally from your life.

What is in your hand is connected to your calling and God's purpose. It is shouting at you! Do not despise or take lightly the gifts and opportunities he has given you. He wants you to use them. God knows the potential of what is in your hand; he knows those things have power.

What is in your hand can seem self-indulgent; what is in your heart can seem noble. Have you ever been asked in a job interview or group setting to "list three things you're good at and three you're not so good at"? Research suggests that the majority of people could list the latter much quicker than they can the things they believe they are good at. Why is this? I believe when it comes to focusing on our gifts and talents, we feel that we are too self-focused and self-indulgent. And this can be the case if we take our focus outside of Jesus and his cause and pursue instead the path to fame and fortune.

On the flip side, what is in our hearts is often attached to a noble cause; it is about making a difference to others. Maybe your heart's desire is to feed the world's hungry or to find a cure for cancer or the like. When what is in your hand is sandwiched between God's salvation and God's grace, then all of a sudden what you do will begin to line up with what you love. Purpose is all about eternity, which he has placed in your heart; calling is about the gifts and talents he has put in your hand.

What is in your hand looks like you; what is in your heart looks the way you would like to look. What is in your hand looks like you because it is you! It is the way the Father made you. Human nature tends not to like the way we look, so we build a picture of how we would like to look. This dissatisfaction with our appearance can cause us to look in the mirror and focus on our imperfections.

For me it is that I am follicly challenged and have a nose that could perhaps have been a notch or two smaller. Even supermodels, I am told, do not always like what they see in the mirror. But remember, the Bible tells us that we are fearfully and wonderfully made (Ps. 139:14).

We can try and build an image around how we would like

to look or have others see us. You may be helping in the children's ministry today, but in your heart you see yourself as the next Mother Teresa, so you are contemplating laying down what is in your hand to join the Missionaries of Charity in Calcutta. I would never want to diminish the dream that is in your heart, but the Lord has made you absolutely perfectly for his plans.

What is in your hand carries the weight of expectation; what is in your heart is unexpected. Maybe your friends and peers have expectations in relation to your gifts and talents. Perhaps your mum or dad is hoping that the years of piano lessons or the 5:00 a.m. training sessions in the pool will one day pay off. When you live under the weight of expectation, you can be fearful of letting people down. The expectations of others may even lead to a little rebellion as you try to break out of the box you feel you have been put in. Those same expectations may cause you to pursue what is in your heart prematurely and out of the wrong motive.

The only expectations we should be concerned with fulfilling are God's, and all he asks is that you start with what he has put in front of you.

What is in your hand is natural; what is in your heart is spiritual. We can devalue what is in our hands by seeing it as natural when compared to spiritual gifts such as evangelism, prophecy, and healing of the sick. Your own gift may seem to lack spiritual significance or weight.

However, every gift has value and a spiritual dimension when you have the cause of Christ in your heart. Regardless of whether your gift is in plumbing, carpentry, or accounting, when you are faithful with it, the Lord will use it for his purposes.

You may be thinking, "Brian, I have been using what is in my hand faithfully and diligently for years but seem no closer to what is in my heart."

I would encourage you first to accept the Master's design and, second, to begin changing. Seek God about the areas, the attitudes, the things that may have created a wall in your life, preventing you from entering into his promises and purpose.

Sadly, people's gifts can sometimes take them where their character cannot sustain them. I encourage you not to underestimate the seemingly little things in your character. They have potency. Do not allow them to keep you from realizing your holy calling.

Finally, I encourage you to begin serving if you are not already. Luke 16:10 says, "He who is faithful in what is least is faithful also in much." You may think that the Lord has called you to the global, but if you are not faithful in the here and now with what may seem small, you will not ever be faithful or trusted with much. Start serving in church or volunteering your time to a charity or applying your gifts in your workplace. Start being faithful and diligent there, and I believe God will open the door to what is in your heart.

What is in your hand? Is it a musical gift? An ability for numbers? Business acumen? The gift of hospitality? Great communication skills? An ability to listen and comfort? It could be one or more of a multitude of things. I honestly believe that we all need to consider what is in our hands right now. See the potential of what God has given and how it could lead to the opportunity to fulfill what is in your heart on a much bigger scale.

> *You may think that the Lord has called you to the global, but if you are not faithful in the here and now with what may seem small, you will not ever be faithful or trusted with much.*

Psalm 37 speaks about the desires of our heart and tells us to commit our way to the Lord. God has a way for your life, and it relates to the way he designed you and created you. Serve him with the gifts he has given you, and he will give you the desires of your heart.

Chapter 8

The Blessing of Hard Work

I WAS AT A WEDDING ONCE, SITTING AT A TABLE full of strangers, which can always be a little awkward. So I began the normal small talk with the guy sitting to my right, "How do you know the lovely couple?" "Did you mow the lawn today? We've had good weather for lawn mowing." "Who do you follow in football?" And finally, "What do you do for work?" It is usually my job of pastor that gets the most interesting responses, but this time, even my job profile was outdone. "I bag and sell chicken manure," he responded. "Really," I said. "Do you enjoy that?" (What else could I say?)

"It's manure," he replied. He then proceeded to tell me what the worst part of the job is, as if it needed explaining. He said that there is a kind of parasite in chicken manure or bacteria of some sort that attaches itself to the lining of the nasal cavity. It is almost impossible to kill, and the effect is that no matter how clean you are or how many showers you take, you always smell manure, and because you can smell it, you think everyone else can too!

Now, I am sure you agree that his job is up there with the worst jobs in the world! One of the worst jobs I ever had was during the time leading up to our wedding. I was saving money for the wedding and the honeymoon, so I took a night job cleaning a large, car assembly plant. I had to clean the men's bathrooms (which was almost comparable to working with chicken manure!), and I also had to clean the cafeteria, which was almost as bad. But because the job was tied to a bigger cause, it did not seem to be such a big deal.

I know some people who really hate work, even though right now that is what God has put in their hands. I believe you can know the freedom and hope that salvation brings, you can grasp and be directed by the call of Christ on your life, but unless you understand the power and blessing of hard work, the purposes of the Father will not become a reality in your life.

Work is part of your innate design. Think about creation.

Genesis tells us that God worked six days and rested on the seventh. We are created in his image, so it goes without saying that God created us with a work ethic. Yet many people are stressed about work and ruled by its emptiness or futility. For others, work is completely self-oriented and purely about meeting their own needs and desires. If those descriptions fit you, you are in good company. King Solomon was in what we today would call a backslidden state when he wrote Ecclesiastes. His heart had grown cold toward the Lord, and he was searching for answers in the midst of great wealth and great success.

Solomon so hated work that he hated his life. Now that is really hating your job! He wrote in Ecclesiastes 2:17–18, "I hated life because the work that was under the sun was distressing to me, for all is vanity [emptiness] and grasping for the wind. Then I hated all my labor in which I had toiled under the sun, because I must leave it to the man who will come after me."

Solomon had no real revelation of the power of empowering generations to come. He went on to say, "For what has man for all his labor, and for the striving of his heart with which he has toiled under the sun? For all his days are sorrowful, and his work burdensome" (vv. 22–23).

Do you see work as a means to an end, or do you see it as a means to a beginning? Do you see work as futile and tiresome as Solomon did, or do you see it as a catalyst or launching pad to the purpose of God for your life?

You Have to Work at It

Many great things began with hard work. The Great Wall of China took more than two hundred years to build to its current length and scale; Notre Dame Cathedral in Paris took two hundred years to build; the Panama Canal connecting the Pacific and Atlantic Oceans took thirty-four years to complete with eighty thousand workers and an estimated thirty thousand lives lost; and the Mount Rushmore Memorial took fourteen years to sculpt.

All achievements and opportunities begin with hard work. Living your calling for the Father's cause is no different.

When I was growing up, church did not look like the church I am part of today. Many churches are growing, gaining momentum, and using their momentum to make a great impact in their communities. All of their work has been built on the efforts and example of our Christian forefathers.

My prayer is that none of us ever grow so familiar with what God is doing through his church in the twenty-first century that we forget that a key to the achievements and ground taken for the kingdom is hard work. Achievements do not just fall out of the sky; they are forged with diligence, conviction, and sometimes sheer struggle. And there is still a long way to go. Many in the world have never heard the name of Jesus!

You may look at well-known people who preach the gospel to tens of thousands in crusades all over the world. It is easy to think that living for Christ's cause is measured by such great events and occasions. The Billy Grahams, Joyce Meyers, and Reinhard Bonnkes of the world did not just arrive by accident in stadiums and arenas; their achievements are the *fruit* of a lifestyle committed to the cause of the King.

Psalm 128 tells us that those who fear the Lord will be blessed and that they will eat the fruit of their labor. In other words, when you love the Lord and carry his cause in your heart, he will reward you for all your hard work. And I am not just talking about what you do from 9:00 a.m. to 5:00 p.m. Our families take work, our friendships take work, our studies take work, and our spiritual commitments take work.

When you commit to working hard, rather than taking the easy road, the fruit of your life will become evident to all.

When you commit to working hard rather than taking the easy road, the fruit of your life will become evident to all. Even Solomon, for all his whining and sorrowfulness, recognized that our labor bears fruit when we occupy ourselves with our God-given task.

> I have seen the God-given task with which the sons of men are to be occupied. . . . I know that nothing is better for them than to rejoice, and to do good in their lives, and also that every man should eat and drink and enjoy the good of all his labor—it is the gift of God. (Eccl. 3:10, 12–13)

We have a God-given task to occupy us; there is nothing futile or insignificant about that! The word *occupied* means "to be busy, to take up one's time, to be absorbed." Are you occupied by your God-given task? Whatever it is, do not do it half-heartedly. Do it with your whole heart.

The Position of Your Heart

Bobbie and I have worked hard all of our married life, but I thank God we have the chance to be occupied with a God-given task, his cause. It takes all the striving out of your work when you are occupied with a task that is bigger than you are.

I am not sure what you spend your days doing. Maybe you

work in an office, maybe you are a tradesperson, perhaps you are a full-time caregiver for your children, but if your work represents emptiness, anxiety, and stress, I encourage you to believe that the Lord will give you a heart revelation about a task at hand. A God-given task will transform the way you see work and the way you see every day.

I vividly recall an airplane trip from Dallas to Los Angeles when I found myself sitting beside a man who told me he was a top-level executive in a multinational company. There was no denying it; this man was in trouble. He was agitated, he could not sit still, and he scratched his head so much that blood was coming down his neck. At one point, he was so on edge that he took the airplane phone from his seat and dismantled it. I was a little worried because I had no idea what was troubling the man. He got up out of his seat for what seemed like the hundredth time, and I resolved to see if I could calm him down a little. On his return I began to ask him what it was that had him so preoccupied and worried. It turns out his company had given him time off due to stress. He was burning out. As the conversation went on, I discovered that his marriage was in strife and some deep heart issues were plaguing him.

Solomon also confessed that his despair and doubt actually came from deep-rooted heart issues. He admitted, "I turned my heart and despaired of all the labor in which I had toiled under the sun" (Eccl. 2:20). Solomon's heart found no rest because he had turned his heart away from God. When you take the Lord out of the equation, work can have such emptiness, but when you see work as having an eternal purpose, it will feed you and sustain you in more ways than one!

It may sound like a contradiction, but do you know that hard work can actually nourish you? Jesus said, "My food is to do the will of Him who sent Me, and to finish His work" (John 4:34). When we get our hearts right about what we toil and labor for, freedom and fulfillment will result.

The answer to the stress of work is the position of your heart, because stress and striving are heart issues.

The Position of the Sun

Over and over again Solomon talked about the frustration, or if you like, the futility of life under the sun. If you are sitting and staring out the window of your office, and the sun is shining outside, I can see how you might much prefer to be out under the sun rather than working at your desk. Being "under the sun" (Eccl. 2:18) speaks of what is natural and finite, whereas an eternal or cause-driven focus enables you to see things from heaven's perspective—from above the sun rather than under it.

Jesus taught us to pray, "Your will be done on earth as it is in heaven" (Matt. 6:10). You can live in such a way that you are completely occupied by a commitment to see the will of heaven accomplished on earth, removing the futility and worry of living under the sun. Bringing the will of God and his blessing into people's lives is a much more powerful way of approaching work. Work becomes a joy because you realize that your toil has eternal significance.

The answer to the futility of work is the position of the sun. When you see work from a human perspective, it can seem very empty, but when you see it from heaven's perspective, it is full of opportunity.

The Position of Your Table

For many people, the centerpiece when it comes to their work is reserved only for their own table. But I truly believe that God does not just want to nourish and feed you; he wants to use you as a conduit to feed and nourish others.

Christianity is not just about having enough food for your table; it is about having enough food to put on the tables of others. Now, I am not talking about cooking up a roast and vegetables for the neighbors every night. I am referring to having enough left in reserve (time, finances, emotional support, wisdom, and so on) to generously pour into others.

Solomon was so self-focused that everything was about him. "I made my works great, I built myself houses, and planted myself vineyards. I made myself gardens and orchards, and I planted all kinds of fruit trees in them. I made myself water pools from which to water the growing trees of the grove. I acquired male and female servants, and had servants born in my house" (Eccl. 2:4–7).

The answer to the selfishness of work is the position of your table and your ability and willingness to feed others.

Like many people today, Solomon compared his possessions to what the Joneses had. "Yes, I had greater possessions of herds and flocks than all who were in Jerusalem before me" (Eccl. 2:7).

However, in time Solomon came to recognize that all his efforts to accumulate wealth, position, and influence were mere "vanity and grasping for the wind" (Eccl. 2: 11). Only when Solomon started to see that work and the fruit of his labor were gifts from the Lord could he be occupied by his God-given task, and his life began to take on real purpose and meaning.

When it comes to work, do not look at it; look through it. Focus on what is on the other side of your labor, how it will release you into what is in your heart and the impact it will have on others.

The answer to the selfishness of work is the position of your table and your ability and willingness to feed others.

There is a blessing to hard work. Do not see it as emptiness or a nuisance; see it as an opportunity. When you get a sense of your divine purpose, a sense that this is about something much bigger than you, even if the task at hand seems distant from what is in your heart, know that it is God-given. Allow the fact that God has called you and positioned you exactly where you are to energize your heart.

I encourage you to learn to use what is in your hand to faithfully serve the King and the kingdom. Commit your life to doing good and making a difference, and remember to enjoy the fruit of your labor—savor the journey!

THE CAUSE
AND PURPOSE

Chapter 9

Living on Purpose

I AM IMPULSIVE BY NATURE. WHEN I FEEL THAT things are becoming too predictable at church or everyone is getting too settled, I like to stir things up a little. I am the type of person who likes flexibility rather than rigid, immovable structures, sometimes to the dismay of my staff and team.

Take, for example, our service run sheet, which is designed to give a snapshot of each service and the order of when things are likely to happen during church. It is a guide for the worship team; it helps the production team know when to cue videos and the preacher to know when to stop preaching!

But to me it is simply a guide, and I will sometimes move things around with no warning. You should see the television team scramble! I can be random on occasion, but God is not random. He is a God of purpose, and everything he does is purposeful.

Everything he created is for his purpose. Psalm 24:1 tells us, "The earth is the LORD's, and all its fullness, the world and those who dwell therein." The earth, the mountains, the seas, you and I, all exist to serve his purpose.

In *The Purpose-Driven Life*, Rick Warren opens with the following statement: "It's not about you." There is no greater truism when it comes to living for the cause and fulfilling God's purpose and vision for your life. It is all about him and others.

> The secret of living a life of purpose is living for something bigger than you are.

The secret of living a life of purpose is living for something bigger than you are. That is what the cause of Christ is all about. Purpose should underpin all you do, motivating and inspiring you in your walk with God, your relationships, family, and career—every aspect of life.

Psalm 23 tells us what a life lived on purpose should look

like. It is a psalm of tranquillity, with all its green pastures and still waters, and a psalm of purpose. The first words of this psalm are "The LORD is . . ." (v. 1), and the last words are " . . . the LORD forever" (v. 6). The key phrase is at the end of verse 3, "For His name's sake."

I believe our lives should look like that: "the LORD is," "the LORD forever," and "for his name's sake." And wherever God wants to lead us, be it by the still waters or the pastures to restore our souls or through the valley, it is all about his purpose. It is about God today, it is about eternity, and it is about every day in between, lived for his name's sake.

Our purpose shapes how we live, how we respond, the choices we make, and how we face the seasons of life. Purpose gives our lives new dimension.

When the Lord gives you a sense of purpose, that purpose ruins you for anything else. Nothing else will ever bring true peace, because peace is found only in pursuing the purposes of God.

For some of us this divine sense of purpose has lain dormant for years. It is little more than a faint whisper buried

allenges, missed opportunities, and hurts that
... deliver up. But it is time for a reawakening!

When the Lord gives you a sense of purpose, that purpose ruins you for anything else. Nothing else will ever bring
true peace, because peace is found only in pursuing the purposes of God.

Purpose Gives a Singleness of Focus

If you have ever been to the circus or seen a lion show, you
probably noticed the lion tamer's tools: a whip and a small
stool. The three-legged stool is key in keeping the deadly
animals at bay, because the lions do not know what to focus
on, effectually paralyzing them. Similarly, a lack of focus can
paralyze us with inaction or ineffectiveness.

Many people's lives have no momentum, no forward
progress, because they do not have singleness of focus. Instead,
things compete for their attention, their time, and their
commitment.

A life lived for godly purpose is immediately given a
focus. There is no room for plurality or duplicity in your life.
Godly purpose will give you a singleness of heart.

Bobbie and I often are asked how we make our marriage,
our relationship with our kids, our church life, friendships,
and travel schedules work together. To us it is quite simple

because we feel we do only one thing—that is, live for God's purpose and cause. Our lives focus on seeing the kingdom of God going forward, seeing his house built, raising great children, and building a strong marriage. At every level, all we do is about God and his house.

I think the struggle comes when people try to box or compartmentalize their lives. One box is the box for God, another one is for family, and a different one is for church and ministry. This compartmentalization results in constant frustration as different areas of your life vie for your attention. The key is to simplify your life by decompartmentalizing.

Your life is not meant to be a to-do list of competing priorities. We have all got one life to live, the God-life. It has God at the center, and all the other aspects of your life flow from, and hinge on, him.

Your life is not meant to be a to-do list of competing priorities. We all have one life to live, the God-life. It has God at the center, and all the other aspects of your life flow from, and hinge on, him.

·omes to purpose, we need to adopt the postage-
...p approach—stick to one thing until it reaches its destination! For us that destination is eternity.

Purpose Shapes Our Confession

Words are powerful, and what flows from our mouths can
either build up or tear down. Your words about others and
your confession about yourself reveal what is in your heart.
"For out of the abundance of the heart the mouth speaks"
(Matt. 12:34).

It is true; the good man, out of the good in his heart, will
speak good things; the evil man, out of the evil in his heart,
will speak evil. When purpose is in your heart, you will have
purpose in your mouth, in your words, and in your confes-
sions. Purpose will shape the way you speak about your future,
what you believe about God and yourself, and what you have
faith for.

The key to seeing the Father's purpose outworked is
having his Word in your heart. Deuteronomy 30:14 reads,
"The word is very near you, in your mouth and in your
heart, that you may do it." First we need to know God's Word
so that our words become a genuine reflection of what is
in his heart.

You cannot trick your heart simply by speaking the right

words; such words are hollow and hold little weight. But when you speak out of the abundance of your heart, words that flow from a "divinely implanted sense of a purpose" (Eccl. 3:11 AMP), your words are filled with purpose and power.

Purpose Exudes Life

Each year thousands of students from around the world come to Hillsong College to study and serve with us for one to three years in the areas of leadership, worship, and TV and media. After college they generally take what they have learned and gleaned to their home church. At the beginning of each semester, I gather our staff and students together so we all have a chance to meet. I love these gatherings because, as I look out at the sea of faces, I see people who exude life,

When it comes to purpose, we need to adopt the postage-stamp approach—stick to one thing until it reaches its destination! For us that destination is eternity.

who are excited about their purpose and destiny. I can literally see the excitement on their faces—they radiate.

That is what living for "His name's sake" does; it is as if God's purpose were written across your face and your life. His presence and purpose are obvious in the way you speak, the way you live, what you pursue (and do not pursue), and how you face opposition and challenges. You have a knowing steadfastness and a sense of quiet confidence.

King David displays this same confidence and security in the Psalms. Even when surrounded by his enemies, David could say about God, "He makes me to lie down in green pastures; He leads me beside the still waters. He restores my soul; He leads me in the paths of righteousness for His name's sake. . . . My cup runs over" (Ps. 23: 2–3, 5).

> *Those who live with purpose always seem to find a way of coming out on top because their commitment to purpose outweighs any discouragement or opposition.*

David also speaks about walking through the valley of the shadow of death; he says "I will fear no evil" (Ps. 23:4). This is very different from saying that there is no evil to fear. No matter how barren "the valley of the shadow of death" looks or how many vultures might be flying overhead, there is

nothing to fear because the Lord is with you. With co...
you can look to the future and know the best is yet to come!

Those who live with purpose always seem to find a way of coming out on top because their commitment to purpose outweighs any discouragement or opposition. If opposition or attack comes your way or tragedy and challenges beset you, know there is a way through. You can have confidence in the fact that "All things *work together* for good to those who love God, to those who are the called according to His purpose "(Rom. 8:28, emphasis added).

Purpose Helps Overcome Lack

"The LORD is my shepherd; I shall not want" (Ps. 23:1). The word *want* literally means to "decrease, to diminish, to make small." That is what lack does in your life. Whether it is a physical lack (such as a financial shortage) or a lack of creativity, wisdom, faith, or peace, lack attempts to shrink your life and decrease your potential.

It is one thing to be in lack, and it is an entirely different thing to glorify lack. It is sad when people allow their real or perceived lack to hold them back from the future the Lord has for them. David knew that the Lord was his shepherd, and his trust, provision, and sufficiency were in God, even in times of lack.

You cannot afford to lack what God intends to build into your life. David could not afford to lack God's presence; Daniel could not afford to lack integrity; and Solomon could not afford to lack wisdom. He said that "wisdom is the principal thing" (Prov. 4:7). These men all knew "lack" would rob them of their purpose. In the same way, lack—wherever it exists in your life—will try and steal from you what Jesus died to give you.

You are designed to live a purpose-filled life. This means breaking the power of lack wherever it may have a hold over you. When you live with purpose, it magnifies where lack is holding you back. In fact, purpose gives you the capacity and the conviction to break the hold of lack in your life.

Purpose Replenishes

In my office I have many photos of Bobbie and the kids, a great painting of a cricket match (a game not appreciated in all parts of the world), and other significant mementos. Why? Because they signify things I love and enjoy, and they help remind me of that fact. Ultimately, though, these are mere pictures, and they are no substitute for spending time with my family or being in the presence of God or watching a good sports game. In other words, what these pictures represent is more important to me.

When it comes to life, we can sometimes look to things to feed our souls or replenish us. We often think, *If only I could live on a farm and get myself some of those green pastures David talks about.* But the green pastures were not literal. Remember, David was running from his enemies; he was speaking about finding inner peace and tranquillity, the kind that only the Lord can give, as it is he who restores our souls (Ps. 23:3).

In more than half a century of life, I have never seen anyone who had a divinely implanted sense of purpose opt out of pursuing God's will for his or her life and find peace and tranquility. That individual may have believed that if things were less busy, if commitments were fewer, or if he or she had been less generous, peace would be possible. But when you live with purpose, God puts tranquility on the inside. Even in the midst of the busyness of life, even when you are out of your comfort zone, he will restore your soul.

Living for godly purpose will take you out of your comfort zone.

There is nothing more replenishing than being in the will of the Father. When God has touched your heart with purpose, nothing else will satisfy. You were born with and for purpose, and you were born for the house of God. Written across your life are the words "The Lord is the Lord forever," and nothing less than that can ever fulfill you.

Purpose Determines What Follows You

William Booth, founder of the Salvation Army, received much attack and criticism in the early days from the press and from other religious leaders. Whenever his son Bramwell brought him the latest newspaper attack, he would respond: "Bramwell, fifty years hence it will matter very little indeed how these people treated us; it will matter a great deal how we dealt with the work of God."

Like William Booth, we may not have the power to determine or change what confronts us, or the challenges we face, but we have power over what follows us—our legacy. David said in Psalm 23:6, "Surely goodness and mercy shall follow me all the days of my life."

What follows you is determined by what you choose to follow. Follow God's purposes, and his nature and character will follow you.

Purpose Is Multidimensional

Purpose is not one-dimensional. When you live with a divinely implanted sense of purpose, you experience a new dimension to salvation, the Holy Spirit, God's provision, your own transformation and healing, and the church.

When it comes to your salvation, purpose gives you a

revelation that "being saved" is bigger than you and heaven. You have an eternal perspective. The work of the Holy Spirit also takes on a new dimension. Luke 4:18 says, "The Spirit of the LORD is upon Me." Yes, the Spirit is on you, but purpose helps you see why! He has anointed you to preach the gospel, heal the brokenhearted, bring liberty to the captives, and heal the blind (Luke 4:18–19).

The power of the Holy Spirit is not only reserved for you; his power should go beyond you—and me—and the four walls of the church.

Provision also takes on an extra dimension when linked to purpose. Imagine you are walking down the road, and suddenly a juicy red apple falls on your head. You may think it is a miracle, provision directly from God. But on the other side of the fence, the owner of the apple tree is shaking its trunk because he wants to bless the passersby.

Some who do not understand purpose can live from miracle to miracle, but God works both miracles and blessings. I believe the Lord wants you not only to be the recipient of the apple, but also to be the one shaking the tree.

Purpose adds a fresh dimension to transformation and healing. Purpose makes the difference between a deliverance mentality—"God please take it away"—and one of overcoming—"God help me win the victory." People sometimes ask God to take away what he has already empowered them to overcome. Sadly, they can live as victims of that situation rather than victors. Being purpose-driven will give you the spirit of an overcomer.

A revelation of purpose helps us understand the importance of change. As it applies to healing and wholeness, purpose causes us to want to change rather than remain as we are. Healing is no longer just about you; it is about building your life in a way that encourages, inspires, and points others to Jesus. It is about equipping you to make a greater difference.

People sometimes ask God to take away what he has already empowered them to overcome.

Finally, purpose adds a new dimension to church. Hebrews 10:25 reminds us not to give up meeting together. If we believe we are saved only for heaven, then church can be about an obligation, but purpose gives church and your commitment to the house of God a new element. You recognize that the church is like a natural body, and every person is a different and vital body part. If you are out of the equation, the body of Christ does not work quite as effectively. The church is all about kingdom purpose.

"The Lord is the Lord forever," and every moment in between is "for His name's sake" (Ps. 23:3). God's purpose unites. When you keep your eyes on purpose, it will bui~ every part of your life. It empowers you, gives you clarity of focus, replenishes and restores you, and gives you the ability to overcome whatever comes your way. A revelation that you were created for a divine purpose removes the duplicity from your life and will keep you on course with your God-ordained destiny.

Chapter 10

Time for Every Purpose

THERE IS A YOUNG MAN IN OUR CHURCH NAMED Grant who has been coming since he was fifteen. He started in our youth ministry, married a girl from church, and now has children of his own. I remember him speaking to me years ago, just as he finished high school, about the dilemma he faced. He wanted to go to Bible college to become a pastor, but his dad wanted him to learn a trade. He asked me what I thought he should do. I told him he should honor his dad because there was plenty of time to go to Bible college. Year after year he would tell me, "Pastor Brian, I just want to be a pastor and would one day love to be your right-hand

THE CAUSE AND PURPOSE

man." I kept encouraging him to stay faithful with what was in his hand, and in time the Lord would make a way for the desires of his heart to be realized.

He eventually left his trade and became a salesman for a pharmaceutical company with a good salary package and a company car, but still, he would remind me of that dream in his heart.

After a number of years, I decided to offer him a role on staff but told him it would mean starting from the bottom. That meant sacrificing the corporate salary and the car. To my surprise, he accepted the offer.

Fast-forward a few years, during which time he did everything asked of him with diligence and consistency. Following some structural and strategic changes, the church had a key role that needed to be filled. Grant was the obvious choice. He persevered, sacrificed, and committed himself to the cause of Christ and the church, and today he is outworking the very thing God placed in his heart years before.

He could have grown impatient, believing his time was never going to come, but instead, he understood that time has a purpose. Too often I have seen people give up on a dream or walk out on a marriage or a job because they felt things were not progressing fast enough or were too tough for too long.

We often feel like time is conspiring against us—an enemy of our hopes and dreams. How do you see time? Do you take it for granted or believe it is working against you?

Time is actually a gift from God. Anything of substance takes time to build, including a life lived for the cause of Christ. God has graced us with time so the purposes and desires of our hearts can become a reality.

> *God has graced us with time so the purposes and desires of our hearts can become a reality.*

Time Is for a Purpose

When you understand time as it relates to God's purpose for you, it will change how you see where you are, as well as where you are heading. You begin to discover that time is actually on your side. Ecclesiastes 3:1 says: "To everything there is a season, a time for every purpose under heaven."

Although Solomon may have been in a bad spiritual state when he penned these words, he understood that time was valuable and related to God's purpose. Galatians 4:4 says, "When the fullness of the time had come, God sent forth

His Son." This Scripture teaches us that God sent his Son Jesus at the perfect time to fulfill his purpose.

Nothing about God is futile or inconsequential. Time is pivotal to your destiny. Each day you are alive is full of opportunity.

I am sure there have been times you have prayed and believed God for an instant miracle, perhaps in the area of your health, your finances, or to overcome a specific situation. Although God could do

> *God will use time to grow, enlarge, and increase your capacity, so do not ever dismiss the value of time.*

immediately what you believe he is going to do, often his answer is not instantaneous. God does not wait to frustrate us; he knows that something significant happens with the passage of time.

Perhaps you have sown time into a relationship or donated money to your local church, a business endeavor, or another cause. You may have prayed and believed for someone to come to salvation or find healing. Perhaps you are wondering when your time will come. Many people want answered prayers, but they do not necessarily want to give things time.

God will use time to grow, enlarge, and increase your capacity, so do not ever dismiss the value of time. Every moment is

full of purpose and has the power to shape your destiny. Time
has a purpose.

Time Brings Seasons

We have all lived enough life to know that it is not all sum-
mers (promises fulfilled, abundance, and joy), nor is it all winters (dry, challenging, and tough). Over a lifetime we will live
through different seasons. Solomon said, "To everything there
is a season" (Eccl. 3:1). By definition a season has both a beginning and an end.

Genesis 8:22 also refers to seasons. It says that as long as
the earth endures, there will be "seedtime and harvest." In
other words, there is a time to sow and a time to reap. A
farmer understands this principle. He labors and toils to sow
seed in anticipation of an abundant harvest. The same can be
applied to our lives.

Ecclesiastes 3:2–9 tells us that there is a time to be born,
a time to die; a time to plant, a time to harvest; a time to
weep, a time to laugh; a time to mourn, and a time to dance.
Whatever season you are in, know that it is part of God's
bigger plan for your life.

Bobbie and I have been through our share of winters. We
have had to lean on God and trust him. In time the winter
seasons have passed, replaced by a new day and fresh hope.

Ecclesiastes 7:14 gives us insight into how best to approach the seasons of life. It says, "In the day of prosperity be joyful, but in the day of adversity consider: surely God has appointed the one as well as the other."

When you experience breakthrough—God's provision, God's promise—be joyful. Stop long enough to appreciate the season you are in and rejoice in what God has done. It is not a time to hang up your running shoes. Keep pressing forward, because God has more for you to do!

> *Tough times do something in our hearts that joy and prosperity cannot do—they compel us to trust in the Lord.*

Conversely, when it comes to the day of adversity, do not become angry, bitter, or disillusioned—consider! Do not over-analyze, intellectualize, or spiritualize; consider and ponder what purpose adversity can possibly serve. Search your heart.

Ecclesiastes 7:3 says that sorrow is better than laughter, because a sad face is good for the heart. We could dismiss this as Solomon feeling sorry for himself, but I believe there is more to it. Tough times do something in our hearts that joy and prosperity cannot do—they compel us to trust in the Lord. Every season has purpose.

Time Is Under Heaven

February 17, 1954, was a great day. On that day I was born in a Salvation Army hospital. I did not get to choose the day of my arrival; nor will I get to choose the day I go from earth to eternity. God holds time in his hand; every second, every minute, every hour is under his supreme authority. Acts 1:7 tells us, "It is not for you to know times or seasons which the Father has put in His own authority."

We can look at time as merely temporal, but eternity is timeless. When your perspective of time encompasses eternity, there is no option but to see every moment, every day, as valuable. You will start to see every situation as having eternal significance and understand that God can use it for his purpose. In that sense time is eternal.

Time Belongs to Us All

There is no escaping time. Despite our efforts to halt time through skin-care regimens and plastic surgery, time passes for all of us. Time presents each of us with the opportunity to decide how we will spend the time we have been given. God has entrusted you with time. Ecclesiastes 9:11 says:

The race is not to the swift,
Nor the battle to the strong,
Nor bread to the wise,
Nor riches to men of understanding,
Nor favor to men of skill;
But time and chance happen to them all.

Solomon is speaking about God-given opportunity. Success in life is not about how quick you are, how strong, intelligent, or even how attractive you are; time and opportunity come to all of us. What will you do with the time you have?

We can make choices that impact the fulfillment and fruitfulness of our time. Some people drink their lives away, some allow unforgiveness to eat their lives away, and others will spend their lives as victims of circumstance. Then there are those of us who have decided to spend our time living as both saved and called children of God, and this decision shapes how we live out every day. Time is a God-given gift.

Embrace the Moment

Think of time as a massive collection of moments. Think about how many moments make up an hour, a day, a year—that is time. The moments, both the seemingly mundane and the miraculous, form the fabric of your life.

God is found in the moments. It took one moment in time, the moment that Jesus took his last breath on the cross, for the presence of the Father and the hope of salvation to be made available to you and me.

Some people can allow one moment to define their lives. They may be trapped by one bad decision or one negative experience. Like fish caught in a net or birds in a snare, they are unable to escape. I know people who have sabotaged their future and destiny because of one moment. They live tortured by what might have been.

Another moment that can transform everything is the moment when a person encounters Jesus. Life's road forks and past moments and past sins fade away, thanks to the forgiveness we have through Jesus Christ. Every moment from then on is a new start, a promise of a new future lived for Christ.

Each moment is an opportunity—an opportunity to be generous, to show compassion, to say a kind or encouraging word. Do not miss the moments; they pass us by so quickly.

The ordinary moments—family dinners, time spent with your children in the park, quiet times with God—may seem insignificant, but over a lifetime, those moments amount to something extraordinary.

You need to decide which moments are going to determine the years of your life. Look for the value in each moment. Life is not something that happens to us; it is something we, together with God, make happen. Often those who seem to be positioned in the right place at the right time, those who are living in God-given opportunity, are those who understand that time is a gift, not an enemy, to their destiny.

I pray that you will embrace time and the seasons. Live with a perspective that recognizes time as a friend, not an obstacle, to the Lord's will for your life.

The apostle Paul likened our life to a race. Sometimes circumstances and hurdles can cause us to want to retreat to the sidelines instead of finishing our race. Imagine God, standing beside the track that is your life, yelling, "Keep running! You can't see what's just around the next bend, but I can— and it's good!"

Do not give up! Living for the Father's cause and living with purpose will take perseverance, commitment, and sacrifice. It will take time. I encourage you to run headlong toward all God has for you; do not settle for the sidelines.

Chapter 11

Prosperity on Purpose

THE ENGLISH LANGUAGE IS IN A CONSTANT STATE of flux. The meaning of many words has dramatically changed over the years. Take for example what King George I said to architect Christopher Wren after he rebuilt St. Paul's Cathedral in London, following its destruction in the Great Fire of 1666. He described it as "amusing, artificial, and awful." Now that is some encouragement! Actually Wren accepted it as a compliment, because in the seventeenth century those words meant "pleasing," "a work of art," and "awesome," respectively.

In recent times the word *prosperity* has also gone through

some redefinition and has become a word that at times has been misconstrued by some simply to relate to the pursuit of money and financial gain. Anyone who reads the Word of God knows that *prosperity* is in fact a Bible word that encompasses much more than money and wealth.

The Greek word for "prosper" or "prosperous" is *euodo*, which means "to be granted a long journey, an easy way; to be successful." One of the Hebrew words for "prosper" is *tsalach*, which means "to make progress, exceed, succeed and be profitable; show or experience prosperity." The noun *prosperity* in Hebrew is *shalvah*, which means "ease and quietness" and relates to the words *peace* and *abundance*.

Another definition for *prosperity* is "help for the journey." This definition paints a picture that I really love. Each of us is on a life journey, and prosperity is our supply pack for the long trek, as if God has packed sandwiches and a flask of coffee for our road trip that ends in eternity!

In verse 2 of 3 John, the apostle, sending greetings to his old friend Gaius, said, "Beloved, I pray that you may prosper in all things and be in health, just as your soul prospers."

John prayed that Gaius would prosper in "all things," including his health, just as he had experienced spiritual prosperity. The Lord has the same prayer for you. He wants your life to move forward in all areas. As I have already shared many times in the pages of this book, our prosperity has a purpose, but it is also conditional. Let me explain using the parable Jesus shared in Matthew 25:14–30.

This parable describes the kingdom of God like a man traveling to a far-off country. Before leaving, he called in his servants to ensure his affairs at home were looked after while he was gone. To one of the servants he gave five talents, to another two, and to the third he gave one talent. Then the man left.

The one who was given five talents unleashed his entrepreneurial skills and worked hard, doubling what the master had given him. Likewise, the second servant used effectively what he was given and turned two talents into four. But the final servant, fearful he would lose the one talent his master had given him, dug a hole and buried it.

Needless to say, when the master returned, he praised the two who had increased their talents. Unsurprisingly, the third servant received the rebuke of the master. He demanded the one talent be stripped from him and given to the servant who now had ten talents. The master said, "To those who use well what they are given, even more will be given" (v. 25:29 NLT).

The two servants took what they were given and prospered with it. They used that which was in their hands, understanding that their prosperity had a purpose. Today prosperity still has a purpose, but it is conditional on how well you use what God gives you. He gives gifts, abilities, blessing, and the potential for all areas of your life to prosper. Do not bury these God-given gifts.

We can draw some important lessons from the actions of the unprofitable servant.

God Will Never Ask Us to Do Anything That He Will Not Enable Us to Do

> And to one he gave five talents, to another two, and to another one, to each according to his own ability. (Matt. 25:15)

In other words, the person given one talent was not asked to give the same return, he was simply asked to work according to his own measure. It is the same with you. God asks you to do according to the measure he has given you. Granted, he often has a different perspective on your abilities than you do, but remember that it is he who will enable you, even when you are feeling the stretch.

God adds his exceeding abundance to the gifts and abil-

> *He takes your* natural *and adds his* super, *and the result is* supernatural.

ities he has given to you. He takes your *natural* and adds his *super*, and the result is *supernatural*.

You Bury What Is Not Yours

> He who had received one went and dug in the ground, and
> hid his lord's money. (Matt. 25:18)

The servant who buried his talent hid something that was not his to hide. His actions are similar to picking up someone's car keys, borrowing his or her car, digging a large hole, and burying it! The servant was only the caretaker of that talent, and he was always going to be called to give account for it.

If you bury your potential, you are not burying what is yours. The Bible says about your gifts: "Every good gift and every perfect gift is from above, and comes down from the Father of lights, with whom there is no variation or shadow of turning" (James 1:17).

If you think you are a self-made person, think again. Put down this book for a minute and take a deep breath. Now try and stay like that until you finish reading the rest of the book. Holding your breath for that long is impossible, isn't it? Even the air you breathe is a gift from the Lord.

We serve a God in whom there is no variation. He gives you gifts, and you are called to be a good steward over them, putting them to good use.

The Issue Is Not What You Do Not Have, But Who You Do Not Help

> For to everyone who has, more will be given, and he will have abundance; but from him who does not have, even what he has will be taken away. (Matt. 25:29)

Prosperity is not just about you; it is not just about greed and selfishness. Someone may think he sounds pious saying he does not believe in prosperity or in having abundant resources, but I believe the opposite is true. The selfish person is, in fact, the person who keeps all God's blessings to himself or hides what has been given to him.

God's plan for this planet is awesome, and his desire is that each of us fulfills his potential and plays her part. When you live below your potential, you are unable to do all God has called you to do.

You are in partnership with Christ to take the gospel to all the ends of the earth, so it is essential that you hold up your end of the bargain by using what he has given you. He will ensure that you have enough to achieve all you are supposed to.

It Is Wicked to Live Only for Yourself and Lazy Not to Desire to Stretch and Expand

> His lord answered and said to him, "You wicked and lazy servant." (Matt. 25:26)

There are two words I do not want to hear from the Father when I get to heaven—*wicked* and *lazy*! The servant was described that way because he did nothing with the opportunity he received.

You may have reasons and excuses for your inaction. You may even be fearful, but the reality is that God's breath of life is upon you. He has filled you with potential, and he has given you the opportunity to live a life bigger than yourself.

Remember that 2 Timothy 1:9 says you are saved and called. You have the opportunity to live saved, and through that, the opportunity to live called. Do not live just as one who is saved! God has shown favor toward you and graced you to fulfill the mandate that is on your life. Commit to living each day as an opportunity to multiply, expand, enlarge, and make a difference.

Greed or Guilt?

How do you see prosperity? There are those who equate prosperity with guilt, perhaps due to their upbringing or religious mind-sets, and then there are those to whom prosperity is all about "me." When godly purpose is attached to prosperity, guilt and greed are banished.

I hear people talking about a "prosperity gospel." There is no such thing. There is only one gospel—the gospel of

Jesus Christ. The gospel contains promises born out of sacrifice, which apply to every aspect of life and living. I believe unashamedly that God wants people's lives to move forward and enlarge in every area, but for a greater purpose than ourselves. Deuteronomy 8:18 reminds us:

> You shall remember the LORD your God, for it is He who gives you power to get wealth, that He may establish His covenant which He swore to your fathers.

Through Jesus we live in a new covenant, but some Bible principles are neither old nor new covenant; they are eternal principles. A believer's resources come from God and, most important, are for his purposes.

The Bible tells us that financial prosperity becomes greed when it steals our affections. First Timothy 6:10 states, "The love of money is a root of all kinds of evil, for which some have strayed from the faith in their greediness, and pierced themselves through with many sorrows."

Prosperity in and of itself is almost irrelevant when it is not attached to purpose. I believe prosperity highlights vulnerabilities and exposes weaknesses. It will reveal what is in a person's heart and character. Money becomes a master when driven by self, but in the hands of a person who understands purpose, it is a servant.

When you see yourself as a conduit for generosity and when you are committed to heaven's cause, you are positioned for increase that brings value.

Blessings in your life—your health, your family, your relationship with God, your studies, your finances—position you for purpose. I pray that you desire to become the kind of person God can entrust with opportunities to succeed, because he knows you will not dig a hole and hide what he gives you, but rather, you are committed and determined to take what he gives and multiply it for his cause and purpose.

THE CAUSE
AND THE PRICE

Chapter 12

A Heart Surrendered

DURING A VISIT TO SRI LANKA, I STOPPED TO
watch a Hindu procession winding its way through the streets.
There was music, chanting, and lots of color, but I was
astounded to see people physically torturing themselves for
the sake of their religious beliefs. A number of them had
driven spikes into various parts of their bodies, but one particularly gruesome scene still remains in my mind. A man had
suspended himself with what looked like butcher hooks
pushed through his flesh from an A-frame structure on a cart.

Obviously, a life of butcher hooks and torture accomplishes
nothing, but do not underestimate the importance of sacrifice.

A heart surrendered to God recognizes the need to live beyond personal desires and surrender the self to God's will.

The apostle Paul understood better than most what this life of surrender looks like. He instructed us to present our bodies as a living sacrifice, holy and acceptable to God (Rom. 12:1). The same verse in *The Message* says, "Take your everyday, ordinary life—your sleeping, eating, going-to-work, and walking-around-life—and place it before God as an offering." In other words, surrender the everyday, ordinary aspects of your life to God. He does not just want your Sundays; he wants your every day!

We all start off life being ruled by *self*. Anyone who has children knows this to be true. A baby's biggest concerns in life are eating, sleeping, and having his or her diaper changed! I vividly remember times when we were in the car traveling to a family gathering or holiday destination with one of our babies screaming at the top of his or her lungs with no regard for anyone else in the car. He or she was unhappy or unsettled for some reason or another and wanted to ensure that everyone else in the family knew about it.

This kind of behavior can manifest itself in our adult lives too. We may not have a temper tantrum when another shopper's cart is blocking the way in the grocery store, but self-centeredness can reveal itself in other ways. Perhaps the greatest enemy to the cause of the Lord Jesus Christ is *self*.

The Bible confronts self-seeking. "For where envy and *self-seeking* exist, confusion and every evil thing are there" (James 3:16, emphasis added). We all need to overcome the confines of *self*.

Which Side of *Self* Are You On?

I once heard about a pop star who boarded a commercial flight with her very large entourage. On discovering the seats in first class were not real leather, she and her team demanded to disembark. The other passengers had to sit on the tarmac waiting as all their luggage was removed from the baggage hold. *Self* can get out of control. Not only is that true of Hollywood celebrities, but everyday people like you and me. *Self* occupies the part of you that Christ wants to occupy. The apostle Paul said:

> I have been crucified with Christ; it is no longer I who live, but Christ lives in me; and the life which I now live in the flesh I live by faith in the Son of God, who loved me and gave Himself for me. (Gal. 2:20)

Meditate on that. Jesus breathed life into Paul, but Paul was putting *self* to death. I hope you can see the difference. *You* are filled with potential, but *self* is destructive. *You* thrive in the presence of God, but *self* thrives in the absence of God. *You* have limitless potential, but *self* merely has limitations. *You* are human but *self* is humanist. The purposes of *self* are directly opposed to the cause of Christ.

When we talk about *self*, we are referring to the flesh or ego. Again Paul said, "Men will be lovers of themselves . . ." (2 Tim. 3:2). He then compares this mind-set with the

> *The purposes of self are directly opposed to the cause of Christ.*

love of money, boasting, pride, ingratitude, unforgiveness, and more. Not a pretty picture. Yet the Bible speaks so positively about you and your potential. What issues in your life are bringing *self* to the forefront at the cost of God's amazing plans for *you*?

Self Will Try to Hijack *You*

Joyce Meyer shares that when she was starting out in ministry, she tried to model herself on the other pastors' wives who all seemed to dress a certain way, wear their hair in the same style, and interestingly, all seemed to love to bake! In time Joyce discovered that God had not called her to become a clone of anyone else. He wanted her simply to be the woman he had created her to be. As she became more comfortable with who she was, she started to experience tremendous freedom, and her story has helped countless people around the globe.

We, too, can fall into that trap. We can sometimes confuse what is God-breathed (*you*) with what is God-opposed (*self*).

Something has to die, but it is not *you*.

Remember, God made you exactly the way you are. You are "fearfully and wonderfully made" (Ps. 139:14). The things that need to go are self-centeredness, self-loathing, self-gratification, selfishness, self-serving behavior, and self-absorption. Get the picture?

God, in fact, needs you alive and needs you to thrive. He saves you and gives you a future and a hope. God has great plans for you as you play your part in his unique plan for this planet.

Self Will Shrink *You*

When I first started speaking, I was self-conscious. I spoke too fast. I blinked a lot and never knew what to do with my hands. I was awkward, uncomfortable, and definitely felt out of my depth. I kept wondering what everyone was thinking. I shrank my whole consciousness down to me when the realm of Christ is so much bigger.

Being self-conscious means you are far too aware of *self*. If

I had allowed my discomfort to confine me, I might not have persisted, and you would not be reading this book. Today, by God's grace, I regularly travel the globe and speak to tens of thousands of people. This would not be possible if I were still imprisoned by self-consciousness.

Self would love to keep you small and contained, but God's plan is to enlarge and expand you. Christ opens you up to a much bigger world, enabling you to see beyond yourself. If you see the world only through the eyes of *self*, your vision will be limited and skewed. Start seeing yourself as God sees you.

Self Has Limitations

A talented musician may claim to be self-taught. That is certainly admirable, but his or her gift will ultimately be limited by *self*. Could going to lessons and allowing someone else to challenge them and teach them new skills take them to new horizons?

The natural ability of a great athlete will take him or her only so far; those who compete at the top level usually have a team of experts surrounding them, people who help them reach out beyond themselves and conquer previously unattainable levels.

No matter how gifted a person is, *self* will ultimately take an individual only to his or her own boundaries. God's plans will take you further. Therefore, the self-confident, self-taught, or self-made person will limit his or her own potential.

God's Word says that a fool is self-confident (Prov. 14:16) but that does not mean that we must live without confidence. The book of Hebrews teaches that confidence has a great reward. The limiting factor is *self*. Your confidence is grounded in your faith in God.

Self Operates by Stealth

Self can operate by stealth. It can infiltrate your attitudes, your spirituality, humility, and compassion. When this happens, *self* causes us to judge others harshly, use Scriptures to keep people contained, and operate with false humility and pride.

Matthew 23:12 says, "Whoever exalts himself will be humbled, and he who humbles himself will be exalted." What is Jesus telling us through this Scripture? When *self* gets inside someone's religion, this Scripture becomes a negative and brings people down. But the Spirit of Jesus always compels people to come up

I once wrote a book titled, *You Need More Money*, but some people immediately attached *self* to that title and could not see beyond it. The main theme of the book is looking beyond yourself and having the ability to make a difference. It is about having enough food not only for your table, but also enough for the tables of others.

But those who interpreted the meaning of the title as *self* needing more money completely missed the point of the book. If you have nothing, there is nothing you can do. If you have a little, you can begin to help a little. And if you are blessed with an abundance, there is much you can do.

Self Will Preoccupy You

Self is preoccupying. It wraps itself in past failures and mistakes and cannot move beyond them. Even forgiving yourself will not help. I suggest you let *self* die, and the feelings of guilt and condemnation will die with it. Then, as you allow Christ to occupy the part that *self* previously occupied, you will come alive. It is no longer *self* that lives but Christ that lives in you.

> *Motivational speakers encourage self-talk, but the best way to address* self *is to challenge its very existence.*

Motivational speakers encourage self-talk, but the best

way to address *self* is to challenge its very existence. You need to tell yourself exactly what God's Word says. Instead of believing in yourself, believe in the Lord Jesus Christ. Instead of justifying yourself, you are justified by faith. Instead of self-control, you need to be controlled by the Spirit.

Self will always dominate and preoccupy your life with the focus on itself. But the cause of Christ takes us beyond our own preoccupation and lifts the lid on supernatural possibilities.

Chapter 13

Living with Conviction

IF YOU CANNOT ACCEPT THE FIRST FEW WORDS of the Bible, "In the beginning God created . . ." (Gen. 1:1), what hope is there that you will embrace all that God promises and what he can bring to your life? Following Jesus Christ is a faith walk, and it is one of conviction.

I wholeheartedly believe that if we begin to compromise on the convictions that our faith is built upon—the Word of God, the cross, the message of Jesus Christ—we stand on shifting sand like the foolish man Jesus described in Matthew 7:26–27.

> Everyone who hears these sayings of Mine, and does not
> do them, will be like a foolish man who built his house on

the sand: and the rain descended, the floods came, and the winds blew and beat on that house; and it fell. And great was its fall.

Some people do not seem to know what they believe in life. They are not really committed to anything in particular, other than, perhaps, their lack of commitment.

Watching the opinion polls in the lead-up to an election or referendum is a fascinating exercise in observing human nature. The polls indicate the direction the voters are swaying, in order to predict which way the final vote will go. There usually are a number of hard-core voters who stand firmly on each opposing side, but the swing of balance is usually focused on those who have not quite made up their minds. As the debate heats up, these are the voters that each contender aims to influence and persuade to vote for his or her cause. These undecided voters are an unknown, uncertain entity made up of people who are unsure of where they stand on various political issues.

Where do you stand? Your convictions are the beliefs and persuasions that ground you and establish the pattern of your life. The Bible says in Joshua 24:15, "As for me and my house, we will serve the LORD." It is a statement of conviction. Do you have the same sense of conviction when it comes to your calling and your priorities in life?

When Jesus hung on the cross and gave his life for mankind, he gave up his right to choose. He said, "Not My will, but Yours, be done" (Luke 22:42). He then died for this cause. The cross means every human being makes a choice to accept or reject him.

Jesus lived a powerful life committed to his Father's cause, and in spite of rejection, betrayal, and persecution, he never swayed from this purpose. It was this cause that empowered his ministry, enabling him to declare with absolute conviction that:

The Spirit of the LORD is upon Me,

Because [or *for this cause*] He has anointed Me to preach the
    gospel to the poor;

He has sent Me to heal the brokenhearted,

To proclaim liberty to the captives

And recovery of sight to the blind,

To set at liberty those who are oppressed;

To proclaim the acceptable year of the LORD.

(Luke 4:18–19)

Living for the cause of Christ is all about choosing life in all its fullness and living every day for that purpose. So what do you stand for?

I Know, I Believe,
I Am Persuaded, I Am Committed

The apostle Paul was a man of strong convictions. He said, "I am not ashamed, for I know whom I have believed and am persuaded that He is able to keep what I have committed to Him" (2 Tim. 1:12). Can you say the same?

Paul's faith in Jesus Christ set the course and pattern for his life. It is the same with you and me—what we know, believe in, are persuaded by, and committed to will affect the outcome of our lives.

When your faith is in Jesus, you choose to stand on the promises of God, and you commit your life to living for him, your strong convictions will lead to a strong life, a life that is moving forward.

That does not mean your convictions will not at times be tested, perhaps in the workplace around the water cooler or at a gathering with friends who question why you believe what you believe or do what you do. But remember that every test is an opportunity.

God's Word provides us with the pattern to live by. God intends for us to have a life that is steadfast and is not easily taken off course, a life anchored by knowing Jesus Christ and a commitment to his cause.

Are You Living by Conviction or Consequence?

Ever since I was a young boy, I knew deep down that I was born for something bigger than myself. I developed strong convictions from an early age. These convictions have at times been tested, but by the grace of God, my life is still on course with the cause of Christ. Your convictions will be tested at times too.

These convictions affected my thinking and directed my choices, including my decisions to go to Bible college and to marry the amazing woman I was fortunate enough to meet! Bobbie is not only my wife (and a wonderful one at that), but we actually know that God brought us together for his purpose and plans. For more than thirty years we have stood on the Word of God and committed our family and lives to him. Our convictions have

Without strong convictions, you will be likely to make poor decisions with negative consequences. This is the difference between living with conviction and living by consequences.

established a pattern for our lives that, by God's grace, has resulted in a long and happy marriage.

Sadly, a lack of positive convictions has the opposite effect. Without strong convictions, you will be likely to make poor decisions with negative consequences. This is the difference between living with conviction and living by consequences. The latter revolves around what someone thinks is good for him or her rather than what God sees as right. This concept actually boils down to what *is* right and what *seems* right.

The Bible says, "Most men will proclaim each his own goodness, but who can find a faithful man?" (Prov. 20:6), and another verse says, "There is a way that seems right to a man, but its end is the way of death" (Prov. 16:25). I think the Lord is trying to tell us something here. The Father is looking for people of conviction and faithfulness who are living for him rather than themselves.

His principles will set a standard for your life—your marriage, your family and friendships, your work, and your spiritual walk—that will allow you to stand firm, whatever comes your way.

In the World or *of* the World?

Some believers wrestle a little with what seems to be a paradox of the Bible: living *in* the world and not being *of* the world. James 4:4 says, "Do you not know that friendship with the world is enmity with God? Whoever therefore wants to be a friend of the world makes himself an enemy of God." But then Jesus was called the friend of tax collectors and sinners. We are also cautioned not to love the world (1 John 2:15), but John 3:16 says, "For God so loved the world . . ." Where do these seeming contradictions leave you and me?

We all are born into the world and live within its sphere, but we do not have to be conformed to the world's substance— that is, its way of thinking and its value system. A person committed to the cause of Christ will impact and influence the world rather than the world impacting and influencing that person. We do not have to live in exclusion, but we know (or should know) where our feet are firmly planted.

Jesus successfully balanced living *in* the world with not being *of* the world. The values of the world did not influence him, but rather, he had a dynamic influence on those who looked to worldly pursuits. Our challenge as believers is to do the same.

The world's rationale and values can be contrary to God's thinking, so we are encouraged to allow God's Word to transform our thinking. The apostle Paul encouraged us not to "be conformed to this world, but be transformed by the renewing of your mind" (Rom. 12:2). When God's thinking penetrates your heart and you allow your decisions and priorities to be aligned with his purpose and plan, everything changes. But you are not the only one who experiences change. You become an agent for change.

God's will is for you to bring change in your world, just as Jesus' disciples did during their lifetimes. The Scriptures describe them as turning the world "upside down" (Acts 17:6).

You are not called to conform to this world's pattern; the Father wants you to be an agent of transformation who helps brings answers, hope, encouragement, and inspiration to others.

Decide to be a person of convictions, not consequences, someone who is in the world but not of its substance. Someone who is transformed by God's Word, not conformed by the pattern of the world. An agent of change, steadfast, persuaded, and committed to outworking the Father's will in your world.

Chapter 14

Living Committed

COMMITMENT IS A WORD WELL USED IN MANY areas of life. We speak of commitment as it relates to marriage and relationships, as well as to sports. A commentator may refer to a player or team as having played a "committed" game. In this sense "committed" refers to dedication and speaks of selflessness, passion, and drive. Whether the score reflects the commitment or not, a committed game is played by an individual or a team who does not give up until the final whistle blows. Committed players and teams have a will to win and refuse to settle for second best.

At the end of my life, when I stand before the Lord for

judgment, I pray he will weigh up my life and say, "Well done, good and faithful servant" (Matt. 25:21). Again, I cannot say my commitment has never wavered, but my commitment to the cause has outlasted the challenges that have come my way.

Your life will unfold according to a certain pattern that is determined by your convictions (what you believe), your desires (what you want), and your affections (what you love). Those whose priorities are centered on Christ's cause will see the rewards of their commitment emerging in their lives.

When Jesus is your priority, he holds your life together. "He [God] is before all things, and in him all things hold together" (Col. 1:17 NIV). But when a person's priorities are out of sync with the Lord's, life comes unglued.

A simple test for assessing if the cause of Christ is your priority is looking at what you put first in your life. Jesus said, "For where your treasure is, there your heart will be also" (Matt. 6:21). We give attention to the things we value in life.

Take time, for example. Where do you direct most of your time? Does your work or business absorb all your attention? How about television or sports? In and of themselves these things are not bad, but if they take first place, they can determine your life's impact. How about your thought patterns? Does God occupy your thinking?

Speech is another good example. It is quite easy to determine what is important to someone by listening to what he or she talks about. The Word declares, "Let the words of my mouth and the meditation of my heart be acceptable in Your sight" (Ps. 19:14). Separating the words of your mouth from the meditation of your heart is tough.

What are you confessing? What are you thinking? How do you spend your time and money? The answers to these questions are a litmus test for your priorities.

First Things First

The principle of first fruits is a powerful spiritual truth. This principle activates the promises of God in your life. The story of brothers Cain and Abel, told in Genesis 4, introduces this principle. Cain withheld his best from God, offering what constituted his leftovers. Abel, on the other hand, brought God the best of his flock. God accepted Abel's offering but rejected Cain's. God uses the same measure when it comes to you and me. Jesus spoke about a number of "firsts" and how giving them priority will affect you and those around you.

First Seek the Kingdom

Seek *first* the kingdom of God and His righteousness, and all these things shall be added to you. (Matt. 6:33, emphasis added)

The underlying message of *For This I Was Born* is captured in this Scripture. Living for Christ's cause is choosing to live in a way that puts God's kingdom first. When you do what Abel did (and I do not mean sacrificing your best sheep!), the Lord accepts your willing sacrifice and pours out his favor on you, provides for you, brings comfort and protection, and opens doors to opportunities.

Jesus said that if anyone left houses, land, or families for the sake of the gospel (the cause), he or she would receive a hundredfold return (Mark 10:29–30). You may be thinking, *How can that be? If I give my life away—my dreams, my desires, and my pursuits—what's left to give back?*

The truth is that God's kingdom operates very differently from the world. The kingdom of God is not a pie with only so many slices to go around. The kingdom of God is like a river. The Lord's promises and blessing are available to all of us.

Now it is important to understand that I am not talking about having a penny-in-the-slot mentality when it comes to God. Putting his kingdom first is not about what we are going to get from God and how soon we are going to get it. It is actually the complete opposite. Putting his kingdom first means having a heart that says, "Jesus' dying for me and forgiving me is the greatest and most undeserved of gifts."

First Confront the Internal Stuff

Woe to you, scribes and Pharisees, hypocrites! For you cleanse the outside of the cup and dish, but inside they are full of extortion and self-indulgence. Blind Pharisee, *first* cleanse the inside of the cup and dish, that the outside of them may be clean also. (Matt. 23:25–26, emphasis added)

Jesus was definitely not one to mince words! When it comes to dealing with internal issues that can rob us of our destiny, Jesus was clear. He said that we should first deal with the things on the inside. This will inevitably lead to outward change.

Sometimes what is going on inside a person can be masked by an exterior persona that says, "Everything's okay." Sadly, in time the cracks will inevitably begin to show. What is happening internally will eventually reveal itself outwardly, and the thinking, attitudes, emotions, hurts, and unforgiveness we are holding onto will take their toll.

If there are areas in your life that need to be addressed, there is no better time to start allowing God to work in your heart. Spend time with him, ask him to create in you a pure heart (Ps. 51:10), meditate on the Word, and start renewing your thinking. Seek out people who can really challenge you and help you confront those things that are hindering you, and find a local church.

As you surrender to the process of working through your internal issues, your external world will be affected. When you allow God to work in your heart, you will begin to see a change in your relationships, your thinking, the future you see for yourself—every part of your life. The short-term pain of working through the internal issues is definitely worth the freedom and hope it will unleash in your life.

First Bind the Enemy

> How can one enter a strong man's house and plunder his goods, unless he *first* binds the strong man? (Matt. 12:29, emphasis added)

The "strong man" is not the big guy you train next to at the gym. Jesus is talking about Satan. The enemy is always "seeking *whom he may* devour" (1 Peter 5:8, emphasis added). I believe you need to determine that *he may not*!

Jesus has given you the authority to stop Satan in his tracks. The Greek word for *bind* means to "curb his powers." The best way to bind the devil is to live according to the Word of God. When you live according to God's principles, even when the attacks come, your faith in Christ, the truth of God's Word, and your salvation will protect you (Eph. 6:10–18).

Seal the back door on the devil; cut off all the angles he

may attack you on. Give him no place, no opportunity, no permission, and no advantage.

First Remove the Plank

First remove the plank from your own eye, and then you will see clearly to remove the speck from your brother's eye. (Matt. 7:5, emphasis added)

Let there be no doubt; I have no illusions that I am perfect. I, like you, am a work in progress, and I thank God (and Bobbie!) for being so patient with me. My experience in thirty years of ministry has been that the great majority of church people are positive, but every now and then you will encounter someone whose spirit is far less than gracious.

Jesus taught us the pitfalls of having a judgmental spirit toward others by painting a vivid metaphor for us in Matthew 7. Imagine the reality of having a wooden plank extending from your eye. Think of all the damage you would do as you moved around, knocking things over and crashing into people every time you turned around. It would affect the way you see, seriously limit your accessibility, and be a major obstruction in your relationships! There would be a lot of places you could not go because of that plank.

Jesus strongly recommends that we first take a look at what is in our own lives before we condemn others. Decide to live with a positive, encouraging spirit that believes the best of people, recognizing that no one is perfect.

First Be Reconciled

First be reconciled to your brother, and then come and offer your gift. (Matt. 5:24, emphasis added)

The Bible does not make allowances for bitterness and offense, whether justified or not. That is because the Father knows that these issues can cripple your life. He desires the best for you.

Jesus instructs us first to re-concile and get our relation-ships right. Do not allow any-one else to rule your spirit, because the time and energy you spend in strife and anxi-

> *Life is too short to live in bitterness.*

ety will shrink you and keep you limited. Decide to remove any root of unforgiveness or bitterness before it takes hold of your heart. Life is too short to live in bitterness.

First Count the Cost

Which of you, intending to build a tower, does not sit down *first* and count the cost, whether he has enough to finish it. (Luke 14:28, emphasis added)

Before we began building our new church building, we counted the cost—not only the financial cost, but also the spiritual, physical, and emotional costs. If we had not approached the project this way, we might have been beaten at the first sign of challenge or opposition. By God's grace, I am thankful to say that the building programs have never impeded various ministries of our church; in fact, they have given new impetus and momentum across all areas of church life.

Did we face challenges along the way? Of course, but we were prepared to tackle them head-on because we had done our homework, and we knew that whatever we had to go through to achieve the end result would be worth it.

There is a cost attached to putting God first in your life; you will have opposition to face, issues to confront, sacrifices and sometimes uncomfortable decisions to make.

Jesus taught us the value of counting the cost first, because he knew we would have obstacles to overcome. For Jesus the cost included going to the cross. Long before that day, Christ had settled in his heart that death on the cross was a price he was willing to pay.

The great news is that our Father gives us the ability to overcome. Philippians 4:13 tells us that we "can do all things through Christ who strengthens" us. Now that is a comforting thought.

Whether you face a challenge to your health, a child who

is away from God, difficulties in your marriage, or a work or financial situation, your faith in Christ and your willingness to put him first will enable you to live with tenacity and a never-say-die attitude.

It all begins with a choice to put the kingdom of God first. You will never come second by putting God first.

Chapter 15

Blessed to Blessing

THERE WAS AN ELDERLY WOMAN WHO HAD LOST her husband twenty-five years earlier, and sadly had never been able to have children. She lived on what was once a farm but had become little more than a paddock full of weeds and rusted tractors, as there was no one left to look after things. She lived in an old shack that was small and dark, and the roof over the bedrooms and kitchen leaked when it rained. She never turned the heat on because she thought it too expensive, and she ate little more than soup and bread. She lived a lonely and angry existence in the last years of her life. One day a neighbor who regularly checked on her stopped by to bring her some fresh bread and found that she had died in her sleep. As her affairs were being finalized, it was discovered that this woman had close to a half million dollars in the bank and her property was worth a further five million, but she had lived frugally, in almost complete destitution, and for what? To give her fortune to a brother whom she had not seen for fifty years? Some of history's billionaires have even more miserable legacies.

I think it so sad that fear, anger, or warped priorities can keep people contained, never fulfilling their God-given capacity. These stories are lessons for all of us. We all run the risk of storing up God's blessings, financial and otherwise, for ourselves rather than allowing God's blessings to flow through us to others. If we fall into that trap, we risk falling short of God's plan and purpose for our lives.

Throughout the Bible, God consistently promises to bless his people. "Blessed (happy, fortunate, to be envied) is the man who fears (reveres and worships) the Lord" (Ps. 112:1 AMP). On the flip side, blessing has responsibility attached to it. The Bible reminds us that to whom much is given, much is required (Luke 12:48).

When qualities such as consistency and hard work bring God's blessing to your life, such as family, friends, opportunities, and resources, those blessings are not intended to be introspective or self-serving; they have been given to extend much further. God adds to your life so you can live generously and have a positive effect on the world around you.

That has always been God's way. He told Abraham, "I will make you a great nation; I will bless you and make your name great; and you shall be a blessing" (Gen. 12:2). God promised to bless Abraham so that he, in turn, could bless others.

You know what it is to be saved, to have a hope for your life and eternity. You know that when the tough times come, you have an anchor in Christ

> *If you treasure what he treasures — people — he can trust you with the resources needed to take his message to them.*

Jesus. You have the Holy Spirit living in you, encouraging you, and giving you direction.

God is much less concerned with how much we give or do than he is with our hearts. He knows that "where your treasure is, there your heart will be also" (Matt. 6:21). If you treasure what he treasures—people—he can trust you with the resources needed to take his message to them.

A Generous Heart

Our ministry has been blessed by amazingly generous people who give of their time and resources to fulfill our church's part in God's eternal plan for the planet, people who know they were born for a cause.

When you know that you are alive for the kingdom cause, you come to understand that you are blessed to be a blessing. Generosity becomes a stance, a way of life that inevitably impacts all whom you encounter on your journey to eternity.

God's nature is to give, and everything he does comes from a generous spirit. He wants to develop that same spirit in you and me. Generosity is not a single act; it is a way of seeing and a way of thinking.

I do not believe generosity comes naturally to most of us. Our backgrounds, outlooks, circumstances, and human nature itself can sometimes hold us back. We need to challenge this thinking and build the kind of life that sees opportunities to be generous everywhere. Those opportunities may include a smile or a kind word to the cashier at the grocery store or a gift to someone going through a tough time.

Proverbs 22:9 says, "He who has a generous eye will be blessed, for he gives of his bread to the poor." Those with a generous eye will see beyond themselves and their own table and quickly spot opportunities to bless others.

This generosity is not contrived or forced but is intentional, bringing with it incredible joy to both you and others. Isaiah 32:8 tells us that "a generous man devises generous things." When God saw that the world needed a Savior, he devised a generous plan. His name was Jesus!

Leave Room on the Edges

One of our executive pastors is originally from England, where he grew up on a farm that had been in his family for centuries. It was a lush, green farm divided into numerous paddocks that would be used at different times of the year for crops or to grow feed for the cattle. Each parcel of land had a name, some dating back hundreds of years. In the far corner of the property, there was a piece of land known as "poor patch." This piece of land used to sit alongside an old Roman path and was common ground, filled with crops that the poor walking by could take from and not go hungry.

An Old Testament passage talks about sharing crops with those less fortunate.

> When you reap the harvest of your land, you shall not wholly reap the corners of your field, nor shall you gather the gleanings of your harvest. And you shall not glean your vineyard, nor shall you gather every grape of your

vineyard; you shall leave them for the poor and the stranger. (Lev. 19:9–10)

As New Testament believers, we will be enriched and we can enhance the lives of other it we follow this principle. We should remember to leave something on the edges so we have enough to be a blessing to others. There are those who live their lives right out to the corners, and it actually diminishes their capacity to make a difference. When we overextend ourselves, our time and resources, we leave little room to move if an opportunity to be generous arises or God prompts us to respond.

The Bible says, "Better a handful with quietness than both hands full, together with toil and grasping for the wind" (Eccl. 4:6). My goal is always to have one hand free, so if an opportunity presents itself, I have a margin in my life to respond.

You are alive for kingdom purpose, and as part of God's church, you are part of his plan for humanity. The best thing you and I can do is take hold of what is in our hands and become successful at the tasks God has given us to do. Be committed to continually building your life in a way that sets you up to be a blessing to others. Determine in your heart that you will cultivate a lifestyle of generosity and, united with others, take the compassion and love of Christ to people, in both word and deed. On your own you can do a little, but together we can do a lot. There is truly strength in numbers.

Generosity That Is Eternal

The power of generosity became all too vivid a few years ago when Bobbie and I were in Uganda visiting some of the thousands of children our congregation sponsors in partnership with the Compassion organization. On that particular visit we were in Kasese, in the nation's southwest. Visually and geographically, it is one of the most beautiful places I have ever been to, but there is so much injustice in that land. We had to spend nine hours by car on narrow dirt roads to get to the region. On our way back to the capital, Kampala, we all prayed for our lives as our driver swerved to miss crater-like potholes. As we bumped along, I noticed an object in the distance. I could see something rolling down the road. There were things flying out of whatever it was, and I hoped with my whole heart it was not a car. As we came closer, our worst fears were realized. We were the first to arrive on what was the most horrific of scenes. Absolute carnage met our eyes as the dead and dying lay strewn across the road.

In such a situation, you feel extremely helpless. We began to pray and bring comfort to the injured as we waited for help to arrive. We all ended up blood-splattered, but at that moment, helping the victims, not our own personal well-being, was our greatest priority. It was a desperate scene, which I have described here as a reminder of the condition of the world we live in. For so many, the world is a desperate place.

That day, we stepped in to offer the little help we could to those affected by the accident, but this act pales into insignificance in light of the fact that Jesus stepped into humanity's desperation, stood up against the injustice of the world, and bore it on his shoulders. No price was too high.

> *Jesus stepped into humanity's desperation, stood up against the injustice of the world, and bore it on his shoulders. No price was too high.*

Many times the Scripture tells us that God is just. He truly is Justice and the cross is all about righting the wrong. Jesus brought answers to sickness, sin, poverty, and all that was unfair and unjust.

Jesus stood between the angry crowd and the woman caught in adultery (John 8:3–11); he spoke to the woman at the well who had been married five times, even though speaking to her was culturally frowned upon because she was both a woman and a Samaritan (John 4:6–26); and he invited Zacchaeus the tax collector, an occupation regarded with complete disdain, to dinner (Luke 19:1–10).

Jesus worked supernaturally and was motivated by the cause of his Father. Jesus gave humanity the opportunity to live in the fullness of God's purpose for their lives. As the Lord's children, we, too, are compelled to be his hands, feet, and mouthpieces on the earth.

The greatest act of generosity was performed some two thousand years ago with Jesus' death and resurrection. Helping others to discover how to live in the fullness of God's purpose is a priority to those who understand the cause of Christ.

Salvation is free; it is a gift that never runs out. And most important, our sharing this salvation with the world has eternal consequences. The Bible tells us that we are called to be salt and light to our world (Matt. 5:13–16). Our faith in Christ is not meant to be hidden under a bushel or basket, but rather to shine like a light on a lampstand, directing people home.

When all else is stripped away, all our earthly pursuits and desires, God will add into our eternal account all those we have helped discover Jesus Christ and his cause for themselves. Gold and silver we leave behind, but souls we take with us into eternity.

I started this book reminding you that God has numbered your days, and you have a few less since you began reading. Although you and I do not know when the Father will call us home to eternity, I do know he wants us to live with commitment to the cause of the King and the kingdom in the time he has given us here.

Jesus exemplified this kind of life during his thirty-three short but world-altering years on earth. He was selfless; he gave all of himself to his Father's cause. He washed the feet of his disciples; he fed them before he fed himself; he healed the sick and mended the brokenhearted; and he stood against injustice. He made the ultimate sacrifice; he died the most painful and horrific death imaginable, all for our sake that we might know him and the Father. It was for this cause that he was born, for this cause that he died.

As the crowds watched him die on the cross in Jerusalem on that dark Friday, God looked beyond his Son hanging on the cross, and he saw you. God knew you before you were born.

Your life is a gift waiting to happen. Your story is destined by God to give answers, hope, and strength to others. You are saved, called, positioned, and empowered by God. He has entrusted you and me with this very time in history. When we live with purpose, his name will be great on the earth—*For This You Were Born.*

Notes

---

1. Ruth Dryden, "Within the Veil I Now Would Come" (Genesis Music, 1978).